CHALICE WELL

THE STORY *of a* LIVING SANCTUARY

Chalice Well Press

CONTENTS

FOREWORD

Twenty two years ago, a gentle journey following the flowing caduceus of Michael and Mary energies from St Michael's Mount in Cornwall through many sacred sites, some active, some forgotten, led me to Chalice Well.

The profoundly moving peaceful balance created by the crossing of these energies on the steps of the pool in King Arthur's Court has spread far beyond the boundaries of the gardens.

Many people over many years have recognised the sacredness of this place and have been inspired to make it immune from the increasing intrusion of modern "living".

Recent research indicates that the earth's energy field, an equivalent of our nervous and meridian systems, is responding positively and intelligently to acknowledgement and recognition from human consciousness.

From all parts of the globe thousands of visitors have contributed to its strength while communicating silently with the earth spirit here, ensuring its continuity as a rare oasis for peaceful contemplation in what is rapidly becoming a fearful world.

What better time to produce a book fashioned by a number of creative minds covering different aspects of Chalice Well, all closely concerned with the preservation of the unique qualities of this very special piece of hallowed ground.

Hamish Miller
September 2008

PREFACE

We had often wondered why there had been so few books produced by the Chalice Well Trust over its fifty years. Now we know. It is a challenging creative endeavour, in which much fine and subtle energy has to be balanced, re-balanced and given flight. However, in 2007 the Trust made a decision to publish the story of Chalice Well in time for its 50th anniversary.

Our approach to telling this story was to assemble a nucleus of people who would be capable of carrying the project forward. At the heart of this process were Natasha Wardle, the manager of the Chalice Well and Paul Fletcher, the archivist and editor of 'The Chalice'. They returned, along with others (see acknowledgements), to the available sources in the Chalice Well Archive and the David Russell Collection at St. Andrews University to explore and tell the story from 'the mists of time' through to the current era.

Different writers tell different parts of the story, and we have chosen to leave these individual voices and styles intact. Regarding the founder of the Trust, Wellesley Tudor Pole, he is referred to throughout the book in several different ways – Major Wellesley Tudor Pole, Wellesley Tudor Pole, WTP, TP and Tudor Pole. Again, rather than standardising his name, we have opted for variety.

We hope that the book you hold here gives you not merely a history but also a source of hope, joy and delight in an uncertain, challenging and changing time.

"Lift up your eyes into the Hills. Reach up to the Summit of your understanding. Look out from there. Learn how to widen your awareness through the attainment of the stillness of complete silence. In that Silence, listen for the Voice that will teach you all things. And be at Peace!"

Wellesley Tudor Pole

INTRODUCTION

London. January 1959. Four men and three women assemble at an office in Smith Square to formalise the legal documents drawn up to create the Chalice Well Trust. For one of the men, Major Wellesley Tudor Pole, it has been a long journey to this point. He had first visited the Chalice Well in Glastonbury as a young man in 1904. Now, fifty-five years later and with the assistance of his friends and companions he was creating the framework to safeguard the Well and surrounding land into perpetuity.

Chalice Well. Glastonbury 2006. A large gathering of over one hundred people is assembled at the wellhead at the top of the gardens. The waters of the Chalice Well and the Sea of Galilee and other sacred waters from around the world are blended in a beautiful crystal bowl. People are invited to take silence and pray for peace and healing for the planet and all beings. Dappled sunlight falls through the surrounding trees onto the vesica lid and the water in the bowl. The rays ripple on the surface of the water. A woman and child carefully pour the waters into the Well. A single voice starts to sing and is gradually joined by many others quietly sounding a note of unity. What Tudor Pole originally called 'The Great Adventure' continues to unfold.

This book is the telling of the story of that adventure. We begin before 1959 in the 'mists of time' when Avalon contained only a small settlement of humans and the red waters flowed freely with the other springs in the valley between the Tor and Chalice Hill. Gradually over the centuries the Abbey was established and a small market town flourished. The red waters and their mystery drew people and many pilgrims found their way to this remarkable landscape. By the end of the nineteenth century the Abbey was long gone and in ruins but a seminary had been established near to the Well. The three central chapters of the book focus on: Alice Buckton, who purchased the property in 1913 and established an artistic and spiritual training centre for young women; the founder of the Trust, Wellesley Tudor Pole, whose remarkable life climaxed with his work at the Chalice Well, and a history of the Trust. In subsequent chapters we take a closer look at the development of the gardens, the nature of water, in particular, Chalice Well water, and also the history of the buildings on the site. Towards the end there are some remarkable testimonies recorded by Companions over the years and a brief synopsis of the Chalice Well Trust at the present time. Within these pages you will also find some extraordinary photographs to complement the text and special features on such subjects as 'The Vesica Piscis,' 'The Upper Room' and 'The Construction of the Well'.

We live in interesting times. The post-industrial age is clearly upon us and we are hectically involved in the so-called 'information age'. Many pundits are looking at 2012 as a moment or a symbol of transition, a moment when planetary consciousness will have reached a certain evolutionary level and humanity will take the next step. Barbara Marx Hubbard, a former nominee for the vice-presidency of the United States, has written, "We are the universe in person. We are the cosmos becoming self-reflective and attempting to understand its own origin, birth and direction and how it can best participate consciously in the process of creation." This process is ongoing around the planet but seems particularly focussed at points of sacred energy like the Chalice Well.

Notably, many of the leading spiritual teachers and pioneers ('forerunners') of the twentieth century found their way to Glastonbury and did work here. The list is long and was well documented in Patrick Benham's excellent book 'The Avalonians.' Fiona Macleod, Katherine Maltwood, John Goodchild, Alice Buckton, Frederick Bligh Bond, Wellesley Tudor Pole, Dion Fortune and Sir George Trevelyan all visited or lived here and gained inspiration from the Avalonian atmosphere. Later in the century came the next wave. John Michell and the poet Harry Fainlight first came in 1966 pursuing an interest in William Blake, Alfred Watkins, Wellesley Tudor Pole and Joseph of Arimathea. Michell was to write that it had seemed in the 1930's as though Glastonbury was beginning to fulfil its natural destiny as England's Jerusalem. Yet by the mid 1960's he writes, "all that was long past. The only surviving relic of the Avalonians was the Chalice Well, preserved by the initiative of the mystical writer, Wellesley Tudor Pole. The garden around it was smaller than it is today, but just as lovely. A kind old lady sat in a wooden hut at the entrance, selling tickets, crab apple jelly and little books of a spiritual nature." However, the new wave did break. People began to arrive. The High Street gradually became a cornucopia of crystal shops, therapies, and eco products – a heady mix of blossoming spiritual pathways from the very ancient to the cutting edge of vibrational medicine. By the 1980's Van Morrison was singing about 'the enchanted vale' and 'the upper room' in 'Avalon of the Heart'. Set a little way out of the centre of the town, nestling between the mighty Tor and the soft contours of Chalice Hill, 'the great adventure' at Chalice Well could take its time in developing. It originally had alliances with other pioneering spiritual projects like The Silent Minute, The Gatekeeper Trust, The Findhorn Community, The Lamplighter Movement and the Network of Light. These links are currently being re-invigorated. Chalice Well absorbed the arrival and curiosity of the hippies in the 1960's and has continued to welcome all spiritual paths to the gardens, establishing a cycle of events and ceremonies throughout the year. The Companionship, those who support the work of the Trust, has grown steadily over the years, and the guest houses and shop have also developed but at the centre of things is of course the Well and its waters – a Well with a garden, not a garden with a Well, as a former Trustee so wisely pointed out.

Whether Wellesley Tudor Pole (WTP) and that small group in London in 1959 could have imagined what exists today is impossible to say. We do know that WTP in his visionary nature stressed the importance of maintaining Chalice Well as a sanctuary for the coming times and this has largely been the main task of those passing through the story. The writer Nicholas Mann recently reflected on his time at the Trust where he was Companionship Registrar and described Chalice Well as a holding place – a particular container of a great body of water – and all the people who support the Well were described as the waves moving through it. He wrote in the newsletter of Autumn 2008, "The central image was of The Chalice Well constantly staying in the same place, constantly the same container, while the people who passed through it, in the past, the present and the future, formed a succession of waves that upheld and defined its shape." This Chalice Well book then is an expression of that wave from the past into the present expressing the love, energy and unity that emanates from the connections available in this place.

The story is published to celebrate fifty years of the Trust. We hope it will remind those who have visited and experienced 'the atmosphere' of their time here and hope it will also encourage those readers who have not yet visited to come and experience the healing chalybeate waters flowing in the Vale of Avalon.

Joseph of Arimathea by
Horace Knowles from Alice
Buckton's play "Eagerheart".

The Bells of England
by Jan Spencer, of U.S.A

Strange bells draw me from sleep
near cathedral walls
where cows make pastoral scenes,
buttercups brim sunlight,
hills fill with chiming.

Impervious to choir singing,
spangled reflections of glass,
processions through transept and nave,
chants for absolution.

I wait at the edge of mist
which measures each rock, tree, mile,
to Glastonbury.
Past vaults where legend buried
King Arthur and Queen Guinevere,
to fern-filled walls of Chalice Well,
this pilgrim's garden,
the receptacle
for my heart's burden of tears.

Above: Vale of Avalon.

From the Mists of Time

This spring, however, was not of ordinary water, it was the veritable 'water of life,'
leaving in its track its signs in blood. George Wright 1870

In central Somerset there is an extraordinary landscape. A broad level plain, once a marshy inland sea, bordered by the steep Mendip Hills to the north and the ocean to the west, is the setting for a conical hill, over five hundred feet in height, upon an ancient island once known as Ynis Witrin, the Isle of Glass, or Avalon. When seen by William Camden in the 1580s the isle was connected to the mainland by a strip of land to the east, and consisted of several hills covered with apple orchards, over-looked by the steep Tor in its midst. Camden recorded an already ancient tradition of the place in his Britannia: "Upon this Isle of Apples, truly fortunate, the fields require no rustic hand, but Nature only cultivates the land." Tennyson repeated the theme of the place being the original paradise or the Summerlands in the Idylls of the King: "The island valley of Avilion, where falls not hail, or rain, or any snow..."

The Chalice Well sits within this landscape as a spring that flows out from the ground at the foot of the conical hill, Glastonbury Tor. The spring flows at a rate which changes only slightly over the course of the year and everything it touches it coats with a rich red deposit due to the high iron content of its water. Many legends are attributed to the spring, not least that it became red when Joseph of Arimathea buried the two cruets containing the blood and water from Christ's wounds below the adjacent Chalice Hill. It is this legend that accounts for the name of Chalice Well, and for its other name, the 'Blood Well.' Some legends said that Joseph also buried the cup used by Christ at the last supper close to Chalice Hill.

Despite the wealth of legend developed by the monks who came and made Glastonbury their home, the facts are that a spring with a high chalybeate, or iron, content rises at Chalice Well, high above the surrounding water table, and, according to geologists and hydrologists, has done so for thousands of years. The water has a rich mineral content, a fairly constant flow of 25,000 gallons per day and a constant temperature of 52 degrees Farenheit.

The Origin of the Waters

The high ground of the Isle of Avalon was formed by the erosion of deep layers of ocean deposits. Where the deposits were harder they resisted erosion to form the hills seen today. The Tor, over 500 feet in height, has been particularly able to withstand erosion due to the infiltration of its upper sandstone and lower limestone layers with hardening minerals. Evidence of this process is provided by the 'Tor Burrs,' hard, egg-like stones that emerge from the ground and once littered the fields.

The same geological process that produced the Tor Burrs also formed a large deposit of iron within the Tor itself. Below the Tor is an aquifer of several water-impregnated layers of limestone, shale and heavy clay, which is being constantly replenished by rainfall. When it rains upon the Tor the water that does not run off soaks into the ground. Some of the water dissolves the calcium carbonate of the limestone and within a week appears at the spring at the base of the Tor known as the White Spring. Some of the water emerges in other springs. The remaining water percolates much deeper into the mineral rich beds beneath the Tor

An old photograph of
Wearyall Hill in Glastonbury.
Inset: Joseph of Arimathea
by Frances Nuttall.

and acquires the iron that has accumulated there. The water cannot escape into the lower water table of the Somerset Levels because of a thick and completely impervious layer, known as the Keuper Marl, beneath the Isle of Avalon. The water in the Tor aquifer, under pressure from above, moves slowly through the iron-rich mineral deposits to eventually emerge full of iron and at a constant temperature and rate of flow at the Chalice Well. The aquifer is so slow moving that it is possible that the water has been underground for hundreds of years.

Although the above is emerging as the most likely theory for the origin of the waters of the Chalice Well, there are other possibilities. Water diviners have reported that the spring has a 'primary' or 'juvenile' origin deep within the earth. Other diviners have looked for an origin on the Mendips, where indeed there are rich iron deposits; some have even thought the water has its origins in the mountains of Wales - that are, incidentally, visible on a clear day from the summit of the Tor.

Spot where The Holy Thorn grew, XXI.

The Isle of Avalon

This name, although claimed by other places, acknowledges the fact that Glastonbury, once an island surrounded by a marshy inland sea, has all the qualities attributed to an ancient entrance to the Otherworld and to the resting place of King Arthur. The extraordinary qualities of the isle: the elevated viewing point provided by the Tor, the unusual springs, the numinous characteristics that caused the monks of Glastonbury Abbey to call it Ynis Witrin, the Isle of Glass, seemed to originate in a remote and mysterious past.

After the last Ice Age, Mesolithic hunters moved into the area, rich for its fish and fowl, and eventually settled. After 4000 BC there was a large population practicing mixed farming around the Somerset Levels. Raised wooden trackways ran over the surface of the marshland to take advantage of the 'islands' in its interior. There was much travel by boat. The inhabitants built circles, mounds, long barrows and hill forts on the surrounding hills. Constructed not long before the arrival of the Romans, the Lake Villages outside of Glastonbury and Meare have given archaeologists some of the best evidence ever found of what life was like in Iron Age Britain. But all these peoples: hunters, pas-toralists, barrow-makers, hill-fort builders, lake-dwellers and Romans had one thing in common: they held the Isle of Avalon in especial awe.

The Mists

Despite all the activity around the Isle of Avalon little has been found from prehistory on the isle itself. A couple of Bronze Age postholes were found at the Chalice Well, the best local source of fresh water, and there may be a mound on the summit of Edmund Hill that was used for sky-watching in relation to the Tor, but that is all. Every local resource seems utilised but not the Isle of Avalon itself. The first Saxon settlement on the island and then the subsequent 'Dark Age' Christian monasterie - possibly even on the summit of the Tor - seem to emerge from a context whose early history is veiled behind the mists that so notoriously swirl across the Somerset Levels. Indeed the accounts set down by the monks of Glastonbury Abbey - by the tenth century rapidly becoming the most powerful monastery in the land - suggest the isle was viewed as a strange place, with special rules, that had an underworld entrance for the souls of the dead. Glastonbury, according to the monks, was "hungry for the death of pagans," and a rite of banishment was required to remove the pagan deity, Gwynn ap Nudd, from his dwelling upon the Tor.

Gwynn ap Nudd, a Celtic deity, son of Nodens and leader of the British Wild Hunt, traditionally guarded the entrance to the Otherworld offered by the ancient isle. Every Samhain, or Halloween, he and his troop of

Above: Old postcard depicting impression of Glastonbury's early church.

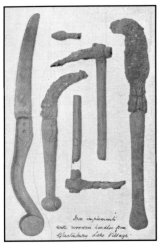

**Top: Glastonbury Abbey
early Declaration Stone.
Below: Iron implements
from Glastonbury's lake.**

fairies, horsemen and other beings – including King Arthur – emerged from the Tor to gather up the souls of all who had died that year and take them into the Otherworld. There, like King Arthur, Gwynn's companion in Celtic myth, they awaited rebirth. In the hollow Tor, Gwynn ap Nudd maintained a perpetual feast with its promises of immortality in a paradisiacal realm. This tradition was skilfully absorbed by Glastonbury Abbey, which by the time of St Dunstan in the tenth century had become the wealthiest and most powerful in the land. The monks of the Abbey fabricated a history in which Gwynn was banished from the Tor with a rite of holy water by St Collen, and the bones of King Arthur himself were found near the location of the Mary Chapel, claimed however, with some justification, to be the earliest Christian foundation in the land.

Partly because of the many attempts to place the coming of the Christians further and further back in time – hence the story of the coming of Joseph of Arimathea and even of Christ to Avalon – the ancient reputation of the place appeared only to have increased through the twelfth and thirteenth centuries. But there was another impulse at work at the time. As the troubadours flourished, as the tales that constituted the "Matter of Britain" came into being, and as knights went off in pursuit of glory on the continent and on Crusades, where else should Britain's greatest king, Arthur, wait for the hour of his greatest need but behind the otherworld portal provided by the Isle of Avalon? Where but Avalon, with its great and already ancient church, should Arthur's sword have been forged and returned to the Lady of the Marshes? Where else but Avalon should the Holy Grail be found? The monks of Glastonbury Abbey grasped the sense of the already ancient and mystical traditions of Avalon, expunged what they did not want, and developed what remained to make the place central to the emerging Medieval consciousness of faith, piety and royal power. Whatever the claims for Avalon to be elsewhere, and in several cases these are very good indeed, there can be no doubt that the ancient and numinous reputation of the island as a place set apart – with its remarkable hills and unusual springs – fulfilled all the traditions and the expectations long held by the Britons for a great spiritual centre and entranceway to another world.

The Name of Chalice Well

The name 'Chalcwell' appears in the Abbey records in 1256, and again in 1306 as 'Chalkwell.' This is reflected in the name of Chilkwell Street on which Chalice Well lies. But the Chalice Well is iron not chalk and the name could be referring to the, then, spectacular limestone deposits of the White Spring. In Greek, chalkos means copper, and chalybeis iron, both are pronounced with a hard c. In Latin calc means chalk, and calx means lime, both may be pronounced with a soft c. Chalybeate however refers to water impregnated with iron and it is highly likely this was the usage employed by the Glastonbury monks. It is possible the words for iron, chalk and a chalice, in Latin calix, soft c, formed rhyming and riddling associations in people's minds.

Chalice Well (or the Blood Well), Glastonbury.

A Massive Grey Stone Building, once a Monastery.

CHALICE WELL is an Ancient Spring, (Chalybeate) of never-failing water, issuing in some 25,000 gallons daily from two stone chambers. The Masonry has caused much discussion and is said to be pre-Roman. Experts tell us it was associated in ancient times with rituals of sunlight and water. The massive masonry is oriented Eastward as may be proved by measurements on Midsummer Day. It stands in a thicket with wild flowers, near to a small garden of lavender and roses. It is about 200 feet above the sea.

Up the narrow flagged way from Chalice Well Guest House the feet of many have come during the long years. Old Chronicles tell us of Joseph of Arimathea, Patrick and Brighid, Aldhelm and Dunstan. The dust of Kings and Saints is mingled in the earth of Avalon, the Blessed Isle, which from primitive times was felt to be under the care of great Spiritual Powers.

Avalon was from early days a home of exalted teaching. Round about its shores we still find traces of a high British civilisation.

The waters of the Blood Well rise at the foot of two hills, Chalice Hill and the 'Silent Tor'—a beacon of remarkable shape, which was a guide to wanderers through trackless forests and marshes from early times. Round the Well the first wattled huts of Christian Anchorites assembled. It is said that vines were grown on the hill. After the Reformation, this haunt of hermits became a Wayside Inn, under the name of the "Anchorage."

As regards the Well, legend tells us that under its waters the Chalice of the Last Supper was hidden to save it from the wild Saxon hordes who hovered on the Mendips for more than eighty years. When at last they entered Avalon they had responded to Christian influence and they left the Sacred Altars undesecrated. Glastonbury has therefore become a singular example of continuity. Stories of the Holy Grail have gathered round the spot from Mediaeval Times, and it has been the scenes of thousands of baptisms.

The Well Lid, of wrought iron and of oak, was given as a thankoffering for Peace in 1919 by friends and lovers of Glastonbury; these friends representing literally every type of thought, Eastern and Western. It was dedicated with prayer and song on all Saints Day by the Ven-Archdeacon Farrer in the presence of old and young.

The symbolism of the ironwork is after a thirteenth century pattern and represents the Bleeding Lance and the Visible and Invisible Worlds interlocked with one another.

Chalice Well Guest House (once the Monastery, now undenominational) is open all the year to guests, with its beautiful rooms, its halls and simple Chapel. Terms: 7/- to 10/- per day inclusive. Vegetarian and meat menus. Large Library. Smoking Room. Hot Baths. Expeditions to Cheddar Gorge, Wells, Camelot, etc.

PRICE ONE PENNY.

The presence of the Red and White Springs supported the mythos of the coming of Joseph of Arimathea, with his red and white cruets and the cup used at the Last Supper, while the growing mythos, in turn, supported the sacralizing of the two springs. The blood spring in the side of the ancient Holy Isle, was a miraculous manifestation of the wound in the side of Christ. Above all, as its importance grew in the Medieval period, Glastonbury with its springs and underworld entrances, supported the legend of the coming of the Grail. Writers, such as Chrétien de Troyes, who, in the twelfth Century, were developing the Grail legends in the context of Britain, found that the older Celtic traditions of the land, especially those of King Arthur and his knights – possibly even the legends of the Celtic cauldrons of rebirth and inspiration – provided the perfect base on which to build their romances. In the newly emerging consciousness of Medieval Britain, ancient myths merged with contemporary symbols to form layers of meaning which were linked with the land. The goal of Glastonbury Abbey with its original 'Motherchurch' and its buried kings, real and mythic, was to be at the centre of it all.

Above: Yew trees today.
Above right: The first Guardian, Mr. Higgs with Yew stump.
Left: An early guide to the Chalice Well.

The names 'Blood Well' or 'Blood Spring' first appear on maps and papers referring to the property in the mid eighteenth century when it was also known as 'St. Joseph's Well.' At that time the spring was an extremely popular place of healing. In 1750 the chalice, or 'Holy Grail' of the Glastonbury legends associated with Joseph of Arimathea, appeared along with the name 'Chalice Well' on the seal of the bottled water taken from the spring.

In the early 1960's Tudor Pole and the Chalice Well Trust decided to sponsor archaeo-

logical excavations on the site. The Trust had received reports that early Christian graves and a chapel were on the site and finding evidence of these would validate them as popular as ever Glastonbury traditions. The excavations began in 1960 under the direction of Philip Rahtz who, again sponsored by Chalice Well Trust, was to later excavate the summit of the Tor. The Trustees were to be disappointed as the excavations yielded surprisingly little evidence of early occupation, but it was at least learnt that the yew trees, which are present throughout the garden, had always been there. One stump of yew over three metres underground provided a radiocarbon date of around 300 AD. Rahtz found that the valley floor had risen considerably over the years, and he thought that the challenges this presented and the small area examined were responsible for the small amount of evidence obtained. Was there more to be found buried deep below the surface?

Above: Well head.
Opposite: King Arthur's Courtyard.

The Well Head

One attribution to the Chalice Well, made by such prominent figures as Dion Fortune, concerns the well-shaft and the polygonal chamber beside it. It was claimed the chamber, which can be rapidly drained and filled, was used for Druidic initiation rituals that involved drowning followed by resuscitation. Claims were made that the stonework of both the well-shaft and the lower courses of the polygonal chamber were pre-Roman. In excavations carried out at the well head in the early 1960s, however, both Philip Rahtz and Raleigh Radford (who worked on the Abbey ruins) thought that the well-shaft was built around 1200 AD most likely using stones from the Abbey Church that had burnt down in 1184. The Abbey constructed the well-shaft as a heading for originally wooden conduits to carry the waters to the Abbey grounds. To this day, the waters of Chalice Well still feed the Abbey fishpond. They also thought that the adjacent polygonal brick-roofed chamber dated to the 18th Century. It was an addition made to the well when Glastonbury became popular as a spa, and an additional reservoir was needed to create the pressure to carry the water to a pumphouse in the town.

A further suggestion made by Rahtz was that the well-shaft was first built as a traditional medieval well house and today, the visitor looks into the building through an opening made in the corbelled roof. The evidence for an above ground well-house was supported by the silting of the valley and by the high quality of the stonework which showed external finishing beyond that required for a reservoir. Later excavation in the area however revealed that silting up around the well head was not as deep as Rahtz had thought, and indeed ground nearby showed undisturbed bedrock after a foot or two. Furthermore, as described above, the stones of the well-shaft might have been finished for an original function elsewhere. The evidence suggests the heading for the well was first built around 1200 AD; but it may not have been built as a well-house standing above ground, nor as a simple reservoir set deeply into the ground, but as something between the two.

The Eighteenth Century Spa

In the 1700s, as the ruins of the Abbey provided the stone for Glastonbury to rebuild itself as a small market town, its citizens looked for ways to increase local commerce. Both Bristol and Bath were developing during this time and the interest in spas was strong. The Medieval belief in healing and miraculous cures persisted into the eighteenth century among all the social classes and Glastonbury had lost little of its power. As visitors began to testify that they received healing from drinking the waters of Glastonbury it was easy for the town to capitalise once again on the matter of miracles.

At the Chalice Well, the Anchor Inn offered lodging, transportation, subscriptions, bottled water with the image of a chalice on the label inscribed 'Chalice Well,' and the opportunity to drink and bathe in the "especial and healing waters" of the place. The healing powers of the water were confirmed by written testimonies on display. One crucial testimony, signed by Matthew Chancellor in 1750, claimed he was healed from a long-standing asthmatic condition by the taking of the waters on seven consecutive Sundays.

Several bath houses were built on the site. The largest bath was in a rectangular building in what is now King Arthur's Court, and there were facilities to suit the wealthier patrons. The flagstones on the floor of the large bathhouse and the slots in them for the pillars that supported the roof on the open west side are still visible today. The proprietor, a one Ann Gallaway, the "Bath Mistress General," sought every way she could to develop her business.

**Aerial photograph
showing Tor House and
Little St. Michael's.**

A new chamber, adjacent to the well head, was built at this time of dressed stone blocks between courses of baked brick and roofed with a brick vault. The new chamber was designed to send the waters of the well into town to supply "a pump-room, baths and other conveniences." This was built in 1753 at Chain Gate in Magdalene Street and belonged to Ann Gallaway. The new well head also served to keep out any contamination from other springs or from surface water. Glastonbury Spa was taking off.

The Gentlemen's Magazine reported that on Sunday, May 5th 1752, "above ten thousand people came to Glastonbury… to drink the waters there for their health." The report said that the roads were congested with their carts and carriages. So many people there on one day alone does seem to be an exaggeration, but numerous records exist of cures. In June 1752, the Gloucester Journal contained an advertisement that encouraged subscriptions, season tickets and offered lodgings. It also listed the cures available for leprosy, asthma, dropsy and rheumatic pains as well as the "king's evil" and "scorbutic disorders."

The practice of taking the waters for seven successive Sundays was, by now, well established. One eye witness, Benjamin Matthews, wrote: "I found a vast Number of people in various Conditions; of whom, some told me they were cured, but would nevertheless tarry the Seven Sundays, which is the usual Way there; and others who were much better, and waiting in Hope of being perfectly well." Despite this popularity, Glastonbury only enjoyed about ten years as a spa. After the death of a visitor, either because the water was polluted or because too much was drunk in the search of a cure, people preferred to take the more gentile, more copious and far warmer waters of Bath.

Yet in 1836 the Phelps' Magazine for Somerset could still report that the "far-famed and wonder-working water rises at the western foot of the Tor Hill, near the Anchor Inn." were used for healing.

The White Spring

A reservoir was built for the waters of the White Spring in 1872-3. The area had been suffering from cholera outbreaks at the time and the town council, under pressure from the government, deemed it necessary to secure a safe source of water. When the building of the reservoir was first proposed, local antiquarians raised an outcry about the destruction of a site steeped in historical and mythological interest. "And what was Glastonbury like then?" wrote George Wright in 1896. "One thing that clings to me was the beautiful Well House Lane of those days, before it had been spoilt by the erection of the reservoir. ... the lane itself was beautiful, for the whole bank was a series of fairy dropping wells - little caverns clothed with moss and verdure, and each small twig and leaf was a medium for the water to flow, drop, drop, drop, into a small basin below."

Despite the protests, construction went ahead. A stone reservoir was placed to catch the waters, which included other springs apart from the White Spring, including an offshoot of iron-rich water from the Chalice Well. The high calcium carbonate content of the White Spring, deriving from the underlying limestone of the area, is insoluble and will precipitate rapidly to calcify any surface it comes into contact with. This fact was discovered very quickly after the water of the reservoir came on line and it began to clog the pipes of the town. By the end of the nineteenth century the water supply for Glastonbury came from West Compton.

Several springs and streams in the area share the properties of the White Spring, and the formations created by the deposition of calcium are known locally as 'tufa,' examples of which can be seen at Chalice Well behind the stone bench in Arthur's Courtyard. The rate of flow of the

Above: Early view of Wellhouse Lane.
Right: Buckton's Orchard, Chalice Well.

White Spring fluctuates considerably. It can range from a minimum of a few thousand gallons a day to a maximum of over thirty thousand gallons a day. It has an average flow close to fifteen thousand gallons a day. When the waters of the other springs are added to this, however, the rate of flow is more or less doubled.

Tor House and the Catholic Seminary

For a period of time after the Chalice Well lost its popularity as a spa, the Anchor Inn maintained a commercial presence on the site. In the early nineteenth century the buildings became residential and were known as Tor House. Although rebuilt with an attractive Georgian façade the building was a jumble at the rear, retaining some features of the earlier inn, including the animal byres.

The property was acquired shortly after this by the Roman Catholic Order of the Sacred Heart, based in France, who turned it into a seminary. The Order built a formidable four-storey school building on the junction of Well House Lane and Chilkwell Street in which to house and teach its pupils. After the order left Glastonbury, the property came onto the market in 1913.

The Vesica Piscis

The vesica piscis was first introduced into the gardens in 1919, when peace had been declared across Europe, and Frederick Bligh Bond was asked - presumably by Alice Buckton - to design a new cover for the well to mark the event. Bligh Bond drew upon motifs from his background both as a church architect and as the archaeologist in charge of the excavations of Glastonbury Abbey. He was convinced that the vesica piscis formed the basis for the design of the key building of the Abbey, the Mary Chapel, that according to tradition occupied the site of the first Christian church in Britain.

Bligh Bond was part of a Glastonbury-based group of people who were interested in a new spirituality that was emerging in the Western world in the first part of the 20th Century. This was partly due to exposure to mysticism and Eastern religions, and partly to information coming from the advance of historical understanding, largely through archaeology, of their native past. Other 'Avalonians,' such as Alice Buckton and Dion Fortune, author of the highly esoteric Cosmic Doctrine, thought the vesica piscis symbolised the merging of different traditions, the union of spirit and matter, and the re-emergence of the feminine to achieve balance with the masculine.

On All Saints Day 1919 the new lid on the cover of the Chalice Well was inaugurated in a ceremony that was deliberately intended to combine all spiritual paths. The speech made by Bligh Bond at the dedication ceremony was recorded in the local newspaper. "An impressive ceremony took place at Chalice Well, Glastonbury, on Saturday, November 1st," ran the story on November 14th, "when a new cover to the Holy Well was dedicated. Mr. Bligh Bond then gave an address on the form and the orientation of the Well and we are able this week to give the notes of this very interesting address."

"Through the last two centuries," said Bligh Bond, "the waters were visited for healing purposes, a pump room being also provided in Magdalene Street for invalids. Within the last ten years baptisms took place, and water from the Jordan was sometimes mixed with that in the Well. As regards the symbolism of the new Well-Cover: In the beautiful hammered iron work may be discerned a geometrical diagram …which symbolised the piercing of our Lord's side by the spear. The intersection of the two circles, corresponding to the North and the invisible worlds, produces the 'Vesica' at the overlapping, and this form is constantly seen in early Christian art as the shape of the 'aura' or radiance around the figure of Christ. It is also portrayed as the outline of the wound in the side of Jesus. Turning to Glastonbury, we find this sacred Well, known as the 'Blood Spring,' its water containing that strange organic compound of iron which imparts a red stain to its channels and receptacles, providing us here with a natural symbol of a deeply mystic teaching, and thus serving as a type of the Holy Grail."

Bligh Bond introduced some further elements into the design for the new well lid. The five-pointed leaves and clusters of berries derived from the Glastonbury Holy Thorn, the hawthorn associated with Joseph of Arimathea. The central line or axis running through the two circles was thought to represent a spear, possibly that of Longinus, the Roman centurion present at the Crucifixion. It also became identified with the sword of St Michael, one of Glastonbury's patron saints. It is possible that the sword of St Michael or the 'bleeding lance' drawn through the centre of the design was an attempt to make the symbolism of male-female balance explicit.

In 2003 the blacksmith and author Hamish Miller was given the task of duplicating the original iron work on the underside of the lid so that the design would be visible no matter whether the lid was open or closed. The two interlocking circles of the vesica piscis are also present in the pool built in the 1980s in the lower part of the garden. Two circles with the sword of St Michael through them is wrought in iron over the entrance to King Arthur's Courtyard. The vesica piscis is in the gates of the entranceway made in the 1990s, as well as in the stonework of the path. The vesica piscis has become the symbol of the Chalice Well.

Symbolism of the Vesica Piscis

The vesica piscis is made from two circles of the same radius, intersecting so that the centre of each circle lies on the circumference of the other. The name means 'fish bladder' in Latin. The central vesica is known as a mandorla meaning 'almond;' in the Christian tradition it is known as the ichthys. Christ is shown in paintings and in sculpture within or emerging from the mandorla or ichthys. The Pythagoreans believed, like Bligh Bond, that everything could be described in terms of pure geometry and number. They held the vesica piscis as the divine figure representing the 'first dyad' or first emanation from the womb of the cosmos. The geometrical properties of the figure were also well known in early Mesopotamian, African and Asian civilizations.

The intersection of the two circles creates the succession of regular polygons, the triangle, square, pentagon, hexagon and so on, and the ratios employed by architects in three-dimensional construction: root 2, root 3 and root 5. The figure also produces the ratio known as the Golden Section or phi. The vesica piscis is therefore a simple, yet supremely generative figure; while the vesica at its centre, when seen vertically, is also considered to be representative of the female genitals.

The vesica piscis provides a simple way of arriving at the basic patterns and measures of sacred geometry. By drawing a circle, however crudely, and then another so that the centres of each circle are on the circumference of the other, it becomes easy to establish all the crucial ratios and numbers of sacred geometry. These are the proportions and harmonies found in nature, in the forms of plants, animals, minerals and the human body. They are also present in music and mathematics, and so form the underlying structures of creation. The vesica piscis is a powerful symbol of the creation and growth of forms in the natural world; and, given the long and successive use of Avalon as a place of death and rebirth, it is not surprising that this supremely generative symbol should appear at the Chalice Well.

It is possible to imagine the progression created by the vesica piscis endlessly unfolding in the inner dimensions of the Otherworld as much as it endlessly unfolds in the external world. The symbol may be the expression of the ideal proportions of the archetypal inner world passing into visible manifestation, and the tangible proportions of the outer world returning into the realm of the eternal.

Alice Buckton: A Pioneering Spirit at the Well 1913 – 1944

To those who watch the cloudy heights from far!
I only know my spirit is awake
With voices of the Hour, whose urgings are
A World's necessity, gone forth in me
To seek the Wells of Immortality!

'On The Heights' from *Daybreak and Other Poems*, 1918

The people who visit the gardens and the Well today are probably unaware of the courage and vision of a pioneering spirit who moved from London in 1913 to dedicate herself to the Chalice Well for over thirty years. Alice Mary Buckton was born on 9th March 1867 at the threshold of a new era. This was a time of change and Alice added her own voice to those who sought social and political reform, including the emancipation of women, and a mystical, personally-tailored spirituality; guided by inner revelation. The new spirituality uncovered common ground between eastern and western religions, blended Anglicanism with Celtic Christianity, pursued psychic studies and sought to express private spiritual realisation through service to others.

Lord Tennyson

"…The material world is enriched by perfection of artistic technique, but the spiritual world is enriched by the muddy strugglings that went on at Miss Buckton's kick-wheel and the spilth of her dye-pot."
Dion Fortune

In 1859 a new railway had opened, making the Surrey hills available to Londoners, and Alice's father, George Bowdler Buckton, was among the writers, scientists and politicians who established a colony there. He was a distinguished entomologist, chemist, astronomer, artist and musician; little is known of Alice's mother, Mary Ann Odling.

The year after Alice's birth Alfred Lord Tennyson moved into the area and became a family friend. At his memorial service in Westminster Abbey, Alice said: "His voice above everything remains with me. I have never heard such a wonderful voice, and it was as rich a month before he died as it ever was…Once he lighted a candle as he read and I saw how wonderfully his face had been lined by the experiences of his time. I remember too walking with him through fields when he said, 'Whatever men say of me I believe in Spirit and the immortality of the soul. It cannot die. Spirit is everywhere. It is Matter that bothers me.'" Years later Alice still wore the cloak that Tennyson gave her.

A Career in Education

Friedrich Froebel died sixteen years before Alice was born, but his writings are as fresh as if written yesterday and reflect two of Alice's passions – the education of the young and the development of women. Froebel (who pioneered *kindergartens*) emphasized the need to educate the child's threefold nature: activity, feeling and thought; this was

At the Well

The rune of the Water Bearer
Ye have supped from the Pools of Sorrow
Ye shall drink from the Wells of Joy!
The golden Wheel is turning –
The heavenly sphere's employ!

A Student Miss Ellis sits at
the well with Miss
Buckton, 1915.
Left: portrait of Alfred Lord
Tennyson.

achieved through creativity, free self-activity, movement and social participation. In a speech in 1898 Alice echoed Froebel: "We shall find no peace or satisfaction if we leave some sides of ourselves undeveloped, ignored, and unrealised. There are instincts and capacities which are part of us from our birth, and they leave us no sleep or rest till we accomplish the work of bringing them into harmony."

It was in Berlin, at the Pestalozzi-Froebel Haus in the late 1890s, where Alice met Annet Schepel, who was to become her dearest friend and lifelong companion. Alice persuaded Annet to come to London to manage her newly formed Sesame Child, Garden and House for Home and Life Training, and, in 1901, she dedicated her first book of poems to Annet, "who proved to me that the human heart has neither age nor nationality and thereby made me free of the World."

The school's prospectus stated its aim was to "form a connecting link" between book-learning and "the practical administrative work of womanhood." Mornings were devoted to cookery, needlework, house management and gardening. Afternoons concentrated on psychology, botany, zoology, singing, elocution, geometry and the history of educational reformers. London outings and walks in Epping Forest were also part of the syllabus. As these were innovations in the education of women, already Alice had become a true pioneer of the new era.

In 1912 Methuen published Alice's *A Catechism of Life*. This was her unique contribution to early education in which she saw men and women as equals and advised educators not to teach sex and relationship education as just part of the everyday curriculum but to make a special space for them. "Every maiden," she counselled, "should regard herself as the 'Guardian of Life' and every youth as the 'Servant of Life.'" Men and women were to regard each other with reverence and wonder, as co-partners of life and all its works.

Alice had been influenced by Emmeline and Christabel Pankhurst's Women's Social and Political Union founded in 1903. Alice took the women's movement very much to heart and, in January 1913, collaborated with Archdeacon Basil Wilberforce to dedicate St. Bride's Day (1 February), to "special meditation and intercession in Westminster Abbey, in St Paul's and in various cathedrals, chapels and churches throughout Great Britain." People set aside five minutes at noon for a week, while a decision on the question of women's suffrage was being discussed in the House of Commons.

Albert Basil Orme Wilberforce, the grandson of the famous anti-slavery campaigner, was to play a crucial role in Alice's life. Appointed Archdeacon of Westminster in 1900, Wilberforce was a revolutionary spiritual figure: best known as an orator, he was also a Freemason, teetotaler, anti-vivisection campaigner and spiritualist. He was deeply empathic and women commented that they felt at ease with him. When he died in 1916, Alice wrote a poem of praise to him:

Fearless and true! thou veteran of God!
Forth-strider into dark and turbulent ways,
Pitiless to the false, and to the faint.

Alice meets Wellesley Tudor Pole

Alice Buckton first met Wellesley Tudor Pole when Archdeacon Wilberforce invited him to present the story of the finding of the Blue Bowl[1] at Dean's Yard on 20 July 1907. On 20 September, she saw the bowl again at the Oratory established for its safe keeping by Tudor Pole in Royal York Crescent in Bristol. She commented that a "great work was beginning." She believed the bowl was a symbol of the emerging feminine spirituality and thought that it would return to Glastonbury and that a community of women would gather round it. This echoed the sentiments of the suffragette, Annie Kenney, who also saw the bowl in Clifton in 1910. On 23 September 1907 Wellesley and Kitty Tudor Pole took Alice to Glastonbury and introduced her to holy places along the Pilgrimage route around the island that they, and others before them, had established.

1   see next chapter for story of Blue Bowl.

Professor Shelley with students in the Tor House courtyard.
Opposite above: The Tor School viewed from the corner of Wellhouse Lane and Chilkwell Street.

Alice moves to Glastonbury

In 1913 Alice bought Tor House, together with the school-building, an orchard, a bathing pool and the spring, from the Roman Catholic Missionaries of the Sacred Heart seminary. At the auction Alice was bidding against a woollen merchant and an American woman, the story goes, whose train was delayed which prevented her from getting to the sale. "The holy well had certain definite value as a source of water power," commented Dion Fortune, "but as a source of spiritual power it was the pearl of great price. Miss Buckton sold all that she had and outbid the woollen merchant. And so the wonderful holy well of St. Joseph and Merlin and the Grael came into the hands of Miss Buckton."

In 1913 the former monastery building was converted for guests and
Alice kept a lamp burning on the altar of the Chapel that had been used
by the Catholic Fathers. This was known as the 'Light of Watchfulness.'

Following the success of the Sesame House project in London, Alice set
up the Tor House Training College for Women. It had an ambitious, inno-
vative curriculum: "Home Management, Gardening, Bee-keeping, Book-
binding, Weaving, Needlework and Embroidery, Missal-painting, and
Banner-making; combined with the study of Heraldry, Elocution and
Legendary Drama." It also offered a wide range of additional courses and
lectures and, by 1929, the annual Summer School included ballet and
Esperanto (encouraged as an aid to global unity by the leader of the Bahá'i
faith of whom Alice was an enthusiastic supporter), and the Dalcroze
approach to music through rhythmic movement and improvisation.
Dion Fortune wrote: "Good music, classical dancing, mystery plays,
readings, lectures, and many other activities made Chalice Well a great
centre of interest, not only to its own visitors, but to the townspeople
also, who owed its warden a big debt of gratitude for the generosity with
which she kept open house to all Somerset." George Seaver, writing in
1958, recalled the impression Alice made on her students: "The charm,
picturesqueness and abounding vitality that went to make up her personality were like a magnet that attracted all who came within the field
of her influence, especially the young."

The Coming of Bride

Alice wrote *The Coming of Bride,* a year after she settled at the Chalice
Well and dedicated it to "those who have heard in the dawn the songs
of the day to be." Set in Iona, Ireland and Avalon, the pageant blended
the ancient Celtic, *Brighid* (pronounced *Breed*); goddess of healers, poets,
blacksmiths, childbirth, dairymaids, inspiration and the hearth-fire, with
St. Brigid of Kildare, one of Ireland's patron saints.

In the play, Alice had Bride dedicate her community at Beckery as a
"home of craft and learning," while at the Chalice Well Alice founded
the Glastonbury Crafts Guild. Dion Fortune recalled that "they used the

Above & Opposite: Scenes
for 'Eager Heart' performed
in the Chalice Well Gardens
featuring the Joyce family
and others.

most primitive of traditional methods, dyeing the raw wool with dye-plants collected from the Somerset hedges and lichen scraped off the trees of old orchards; and spinning it with the pre-historic spindle instead of the medieval wheel... It was a fascinating sight to see the dye-pot boiling over a fire of sticks in the orchard, and skein after skein of gaily coloured wool hanging to dry on the gnarled old trees. ...The material world is enriched by perfection of artistic technique, but the spiritual world is enriched by the muddy strugglings that went on at Miss Buckton's kick-wheel and the spilth of her dye-pot."

The college didn't thrive, and Alice concentrated on Chalice Well Hostel. "Simply fitted for pilgrims and travellers" the former school building accommodated forty-nine paying guests and had a 3,000 book library. Alice also ran the 'Beauties Bower' project which devoted a room to "give a country holiday to tired workers from one of our great cities."

Theatre at the Well

Alice established the Guild of Festival Players and built the 'People's Orchard Theatre' in what is now called the Cress Field. The Mayor of Bath placed the foundation stone for the stage in September 1920. The poetic drama of the theatre provided the ideal artistic medium for Alice, who in her opening speech of the theatre said that "drama was great before there were professionals, drama is the supreme communal Art, very independent, yet full of fellow-feeling and give and take. Every possible capacity and craft finds a home within it. It is a great educator... Every capacity for music, dance, song, colour, ingenuity and resource has a place in the people's drama."

Alice Buckton's major perfomance staged at Chalice Well was *Eagerheart*. Dion Fortune described the play as Alice's *magnum opus,* and that it "occupied a unique place in the modern English theatre." The play takes place in present time but in a world that is not quite this. Eager Heart's sisters, Eager Sense and Eager Fame, not sharing the heroine's faith, go to a banquet to watch for the coming 'king' while Eager Heart, Cinderella-like, is rewarded for her faith in the appearance of the 'Holy Family' on Christmas Eve.

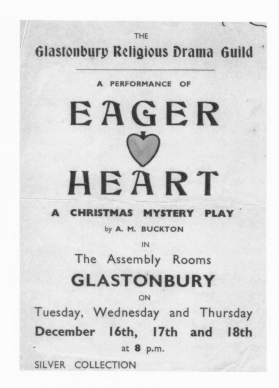

THE
Glastonbury Religious Drama Guild

A PERFORMANCE OF

EAGER ♥ HEART

A CHRISTMAS MYSTERY PLAY
by A. M. BUCKTON
IN
The Assembly Rooms
GLASTONBURY
ON
Tuesday, Wednesday and Thursday
December 16th, 17th and 18th
at **8** p.m.
SILVER COLLECTION

INSCRIBED TO ALL WHO SEE AND WORSHIP THE ONE IN THE MANY

Illustration by Horace Knowles from First Edition of "Eager Heart".

In the subsequent drama the character of the Old Shepherd encourages the other shepherds to "follow the sign with Eager Heart," but the First Shepherd voices another view:

But whither?
Hunger and riches everywhere
Divide the land, like great uncleanly birds,
Gloating on offal! Half the world is full,
Fat with excess: the other half naked!

The debate between the Kings is as relevant today as that of the Shepherds. The Third King is young and described as wearing the "spiked circlet of Inspiration." The Old King describes how his work has been to create unity:
Offering incense at the woodland shrine
Of every god and demon – joining hands
With them that hate each other, and would tear
Each other's altars down – not seeing, all,
The one Form loved of every secret soul,
That all do homage to – the LORD of HEARTS!

Alice Buckton drew in the whole community to participate in or make costumes for her dramas. As an insight into her methods, in her 1915 diary of the Chalice Well Summer School, a student, Miss S. Rees, recounted how Alice came to cast the Old Shepherd: "She was riding in an omnibus one day and sitting opposite to her was a remarkable old gentleman with a fine head just like Tennyson. Miss Buckton knew the latter poet well and she was certain this old man must be some relation of his. At the same time she felt that he was the very person for the shepherd for whom she was searching. She asked him if he was a relation of Tennyson's and he answered that he was a cousin but that he had never seen him. He was told all about Eager Heart and was most anxious to take the part of the old shepherd."

Alice's "Christmas Mystery Play" *Eagerheart* skilfully combined the beliefs of her Anglican upbringing with what some have referred to as a "mystical pantheism." "A Christmas Play normally reveals little of the philosophical or metaphysical outlook of its author," wrote Patrick Benham in *The Avalonians*. "But, ever the wise teacher, Alice Buckton conjures through the dialogue images of her perception of the path to spiritual fulfilment. It is radical, subtle and even – in its way – revolutionary. The emphasis is on heart rather than mind; inner response rather than theological doctrine; intuition rather than intellect. …The spiritual awakening of the *heart* is the key to the transformation of, first, the psyche, then society, and finally the whole world."

Translated into several languages, *Eagerheart* has been performed all over the world, including to the Allies during WWI in France; Alice herself oversaw the 1911 New York and Boston productions. In 1924 Sir Arthur Carlton (a famous theatre and cinema owner of the day) wrote to Alice saying, "it ought to make a most excellent film."

Throughout the 1920s there were frequent dramatic productions at the Chalice Well including a Masque called 'The Garden of Many Waters.' Towards the end of this period Alice devised and directed the Glastonbury Pageant which described the legends and history of Glastonbury throughout the ages. This was caught on film and the remaining fragments were shown at Strode Theatre in Street in 2005.

The Bahá'í Faith

Alice dedicated Eager Heart "to all who see and worship the One in the Many;" an inscription that would have been dear to the heart of 'Abdu'l-Bahá, who saw the play (the first he had ever seen) on his first visit to London in 1911. 'Abdu'l-Bahá was the son and spiritual successor of Bahá'u'lláh (1817-1892), the Persian founder of the Bahá'í faith. Bahá'í was the fastest growing religion on the planet at the time and its messages of universal peace and brotherhood, the underlying unity of all religions, and the equality of women were dear to Alice. It was reported that when 'Abdu'l-Bahá saw the play he wept during the performance.

Abdu'l-bahá, son of the founder of the Bahá'i faith and friend of Alice Buckton and Wellesley Tudor Pole.

On the same visit to England in 1911, after fifty-six years of exile and imprisonment, 'Abdu'l-Bahá was invited by Archdeacon Wilberforce to speak at St. John's, Westminster. The Bahá'í leader once again emphasised the essential unity of religion: "All the Prophets and Messengers have come from one Holy Spirit and bear the Message of God, fitted to the age in which they appear." Alice Buckton was described as an 'earnest visitor' at these London gatherings. "On the afternoon of September 9th," wrote the Bahá'í Publishing Trust in *'Abdu'l-Bahá in London,* "a number of working women of the Passmore Edwards' Settlement, who were spending their holidays with Miss Schepel and Miss Buckton at Vanners, in Byfleet, a village some twenty miles out of London, had the great privilege of meeting 'Abdu'l-Bahá." On 23 September 'The Master' travelled to Bristol and blessed the blue bowl in Clifton and, in April, Alice accompanied him to Scotland.

The Meeting in the Gate

"Within its doors the rigid castes of India melted away, the racial prejudice of Jew, Christian and Muhammadan became less than a memory; and every convention save the essential law of warm hearts and aspiring minds broke down, banned and forbidden by the unifying sympathy of the master of the house. It was like a King Arthur and the Round Table…but an Arthur who knighted women as well as men, and sent them away not with the sword but with the Word."
Horace Holley, *The Modern Social Religion writing of 'Abdu'l-Bahá's welcome in Akka.*

Alice's short play, *The Meeting in the Gate,* reflected the Bahá'í teachings. In 1095 Pope Urban II recommended waging a 'holy war against the Saracens,' and launched the First Crusade. Alice Buckton's play was set outside the Jaffa Gate in Jerusalem. The story of Christians, Jews and Saracens discovering an affinity was a call for religious unity. The opening speech of the play incorporated lines from the poet Omar Khayyám (1048 to 1131) and reminded the audience of the prophecy that, when a representative of each religion met at the Gate, change would occur. Over the years, Alice Buckton kept her links with the Bahá'í movement and in 1920 her name was included in the list of Bahá'í followers with UK voting rights.

Poetry

Her first book of poems, *Through Human Eyes,* was published in 1901.
Three years later came *The Burden of Engela,* a ballad epic, set in the
Transvaal during the Boer War, about Dutch and Huguenot farmers
who had left their homelands in search of religious freedom. A third
book of poems was published in 1908 entitled *Songs of Joy.*

The 1918 volume *Daybreak,* was inscribed to "The Watchers of Avalon
and to all who dare to turn the rim of the Golden Wheel." By this time
Alice was far more of a mystic and the influence of Celtic mythology
had become apparent in her work.

At first sight Alice's poetry may appear dated or over-written, but, her
gifts as a dramatist and her musical sensitivity flowed into her poetry, and
when read aloud, it springs to life. Her poetry is sprinkled with imagery
which, when spoken, leaps off the page. In *After the Gale,* an unpublished
poem from 1930 we find:

> The wind fell at eve…
> And lo, adown the solitary walk,
> Mid crumpled fern and ruined stalk,
> (The penance path of wintry days),
> A tear-lit flaming birth
> Of wakening crocus
> Gushing from the earth,
> In breathless praise!

The 1917 edition of the *Oxford Book of Mystical Verse* covers five centuries
of poetry "containing intimations of a consciousness wider and deeper
than the normal." Two of Alice's poems, *The Great Response* and *Before the
Dawn,* earned a place in this publication.

**Alice Buckton and friends in
the garden at Chalice Well.**

"Seeking thine intercourse
I wander wide
O'er hills and valleys, under moon and stars,
Rapt in a secret tumult of delight
At every passing cloud, and changing light
On stream and mountain side."

The Great Response

Alice's choice of subjects was wide; and included the people who inspired her: Einstein, Faraday, Marie Curie, Pavlova, Darwin, Kipling and her fellow mystic poet and novelist, Mary Webb. She embraced current affairs, writing poems, for example, about a mining disaster and the 1931 earthquake in New Zealand. Alice also delighted in dedicating her poetry to people such as Paul Robeson and Francis Younghusband, inscribing her poem, *The Weaver's Holiday* to "the author of Towards Democracy, my friend, Edward Carpenter." Carpenter was a radical socialist poet, philosopher, mystic, vegetarian, and pioneering campaigner for sexual equality.

Alice wrote many hymns of praise to nature, to the seasons and the specific months of the year. Some of these are heartbreaking in their empathic quality. Her closest companion and co-worker Annet Schepel died in 1931 and her death left Alice bereft. "My heart is bare of mirth and pride," Alice wrote, "The fields are bare of sheaves, and tears, like rain, on every side are falling from the leaves." An ecstatic mystical absorption is sometimes addressed to the soul and sometimes to the omnipresent sacredness she sensed so deeply. Several of her poems take the form of prayers:

Before Sleep   (to be said softly)

Into Thy keeping, Lord of Love!
I give my heart!
Into Thy keeping, Lord of Life!
I give my soul!
Into Thy keeping, Lord of Joy!
My every part
I give thee! Keep it whole!

Miss Buckton in the garden showing the house that stood between Tor School and May Cottages.

Last days at Chalice Well

Throughout her time at Chalice Well Alice Buckton managed to purchase property to safeguard the area around the Well. In December 1926 she purchased May Cottage for £400 and in 1927 she bought 87 and 89 Chilkwell Street (Vine Cottage and Little St Michael's) and the land known as the 'Fairfield' at the foot of the Tor. One of her ventures included opening a tea room, the 'Pilgrim's Rest' in the Fairfield. She also ran the Corner Shop close to the Market Cross where she sold items made at the Chalice Well. The shop also had a library and a sanctuary known as the 'Prayer Room.' As the years went by, however, none of these ventures were particularly successful and financial pressure began to take its toll.

Harry Carter, a Glastonbury resident, remembered Alice in her later years as: "An untidy eccentric old lady with a stooped figure, wispy hair and a very kind, lined face, wearing a baggy old skirt and black wrinkled stockings. She often wore a massive straw hat with a veil, or a black cloak green with age that was said to have belonged to the poet Tennyson. She helped everyone, every lame duck. She was surrounded by theatricals, singers and so on, who came to stay with her – she was always a soft touch! She seemed to have money when she first came to Glastonbury, but she had nothing by the time she left. She gave all she had."

Alice never charged for the shows she staged at the Well and financial problems continued to dog her latter days. In a letter to her cousin, she wrote that she had only £1 7s left in the bank. "The Bank manager," she added, "is not 'one of us;' he distresses me with irate letters." She kept odd hours, often writing 'til early morning in a hut in the orchard and sleeping through the morning. Meals were brought to her, but she often left them untouched.

The Next Step

Alice spent her last days at the home of her friend Mrs. Ethel Kenney, whom she met volunteering for the Red Cross, at 5 Vicars Close in

'Why should I fear to die that was not afraid to be born'

Wells. She died on the 10th December 1944. Her funeral was held in Wells Cathedral. She was cremated in Bristol and her ashes were scattered on Glastonbury Tor. The vicar of St. John's, Glastonbury, speaking at her memorial service said, "She was a genius, a most remarkable personality. Her mind was as wide as her heart. Gifted also with a musical voice, a strong will, the keenest intelligence, an extraordinarily critical judgment, and an extraordinary capacity for forgiveness, and unfailing enthusiasm, she managed to accomplish things where other people would have been daunted." A plaque to her memory is on the wall beside the main door of St John's.

Typically, Alice had already written an unpublished meditation on death called *The Next Step*. This is the final verse:

"there is a spiritual element in many of these poems, along with her love of nature which combine to make her see God in all things."
Rosemary Harris,
Chalice Well Newsletter 1982,

Why should I fear to die that was not afraid to be born?

Why be loth to come in another place and sphere,

Simple although it be, that have found this earth so fair,

Full in the promise of life – great in the school of love?

As a blade of grass I was happy, who knew of its joy as a man!

For all Things travel surely, each in its lot divine;

And all Things move to take the place they can fill, and I –

That know of no other glory, I shall awake in mine!

A Dream of Heaven

"A dream of heaven was brought a little nearer to earth at Chalice Well during its hey-day… the spirit of the place lives on and does not die, for it does not belong to any person, but uses persons to its ends."
Dion Fortune *Avalon of the Heart*

WTP at the Well head
1959.

A Life of Wellesley Tudor Pole the Founder

"Who was he really? I don't know. Nobody in his last life ever knew for certain.
Once he wrote in a letter to me: 'I come and go when summoned so to do; but the human race is not my race. I try hard, with the deepest compassion I can muster, to identify myself with human problems, joys and sorrows, but this is not my planet. I am a modest and anonymous ambassador from elsewhere, give it a thought and tell me who you are. Then perhaps WTP may respond.'"
Rosamond Lehmann from a talk 30th November 1971

It was fourteen years after Alice Buckton's death when Wellesley Tudor Pole asked his friends and companions in the Big Ben Council, which ran the Silent Minute, to help him secure the Chalice Well and surrounding land. It was twenty-five years after Tudor Pole's experience in the mountains around Jerusalem in December 1917 that on an Armistice Sunday in 1940 the Silent Minute was inaugurated on the BBC. And it was fifty-five years between Tudor Pole's first visit to Chalice well in 1904 and the founding of the Chalice Well Trust in January 1959. In the imagination of Tudor Pole ideas would take shape and lay dormant, sometimes for many years, before re-emerging to fruition to establish powerful realities in our world.

Family background and awakenings

Wellesley Tudor Pole was born in Weston-super-Mare on 23rd April 1884 to Thomas and Kate Pole. Thomas was a partner in large grain business in Bristol and was interested in the emerging Theosophical Movement and Fabianism, while the couple embraced an open approach to spirituality. They had five children; Mary Tudor, Dorothy (who died as a child), Katharine Tudor (Kitty), Wellesley (WTP), and Alexander Cecil.

Katharine wrote of Wellesley's developing spiritual powers for Oliver

Villiers in his 'Appreciation and Valuation of WTP':
'He was the first boy after three girls and so was greatly welcomed, but he was a difficult little chap because of being psychic and, of course, he was not understood and so had a frustrating childhood and was very unhappy as a boarder at Blundell's School in Devon. TP was first aware of his psychic faculties when he saw the colour of prayers rising up in churches. When he was about eighteen he had typhoid, I think, or diphtheria and remembered being outside his body.'

Under pressure from his father Tudor Pole turned down a chance of university education to join the family grain business, Chamberlain, Pole and Co., and it was soon after starting work in Bristol with his father that he had a revelatory dream about Glastonbury. It was 1902 and Tudor Pole was just eighteen years old. He was already being magnetised towards the mysteries of Avalon and he began to visit Glastonbury on pilgrimage twice a year to explore the landscape. To his surprise he recognised every inch.

The Sapphire Blue Bowl

During one of these visits, in 1904, he had a strong impression "that some wonderful find would come to light" which would link the founder of the Christian faith with the present time and the re-emergence of a true spirituality for the new century. He asked a priest called Father Field to watch events and report anything that occurred. While on a further pilgrimage, having visited the Well in the valley between the Tor and Chalice Hill, WTP was so affected by the atmosphere around the Well that he knew one day he would be given the opportunity to restore the site.

At the end of 1904 Tudor Pole took his sister Katharine to Glastonbury for the first time. Towards the end of the following year he met Miss Janet and Miss Christine Allen, whom he recognised would, with Katharine, make up a triad of three maidens who would undertake any spiritual work that was forthcoming. In the early part of 1906 Tudor Pole went to Glastonbury with the intention of searching the pilgrimage route for

Above: Tudor Pole in his early twenties.
Below: Kitty Tudor Pole.

Janet (far left) and Christine Allen in white (front) with their family.

some precious or holy object but nothing came of it.

Twenty years earlier, in 1885, a Dr. John Goodchild of Bath had seen a remarkable blue glass bowl for sale in a shop window in Bordighera, Italy. He was able to purchase the bowl and a similar looking platter for £6 and brought them back to his father in England. It was said, although this was later disputed as a red herring, that the bowl had been bricked up within the walls of an old building being demolished at Albenga, a village near to Bordighera. Goodchild's father was immediately convinced that the bowl was a vessel of some significance and it was locked away.

Two years later Goodchild Jnr. had an experience in Italy (a vision) that told him to take the bowl to a certain place in Glastonbury as soon as possible after his father's death. A few weeks later his father died. Goodchild's sister brought the bowl and platter to Italy in the spring of 1898 and Goodchild kept the bowl and sent the platter (thought to be of later origin) to a prominent Italian family. On the 1st of September 1898 he placed the bowl under a stone in a water-filled muddy sluice near Bride's Mound in Glastonbury on the existing pilgrim route.

From 1898 to 1906 Goodchild made pilgrimage to the spot every year (except 1905) and became convinced that the bowl was no longer there. There is some evidence that he came into contact with WTP during this period but both parties pledged that the bowl was never mentioned. In fact, Goodchild only ever mentioned the Bowl to one person, William Sharp (aka Fiona Macleod) who composed the lines:

'From the Silence of Time, Time's Silence Borrow
In the heart of Today is the word of Tomorrow.
The Builders of Joy are the Children of Sorrow,'
on a visit to Glastonbury with Goodchild.

Early in 1906, while working in his office in Bristol, WTP was shown a vision of the whereabouts of a significant object that was to be retrieved from the ground. On 3rd September 1906 the Allen sisters came to find it. They visited the sluice, already a shrine site on the Glastonbury pilgrimage route that seems to have existed previously in an oral tradition. They cleared away the mud and found the glass bowl. Amazed by its beauty and feeling of great sanctity, they washed it, replaced it and returned to Bristol. There followed some contact by letter and in person with Dr. Goodchild and on 1st of October 1906 at Wellesley's request Kitty Tudor Pole went to Glastonbury, retrieved the vessel and took it back to Tudor Pole's house in Bristol where they had prepared a shrine at the top of his house in Royal York Crescent.

So began WTP's first big spiritual adventure, which would eventually lead him to place the bowl in the care of the Chalice Well Trust in 1968. From 1906 to 1914 the bowl remained in the small Oratory at Clifton and until the end of 1908 this sanctuary was open to all visitors. Early in 1909 they were forced to close the Oratory due to overwhelming interest, sparked mainly by a meeting in Dean's Yard, London in July 1907. At the meeting, attended by over fifty luminaries including Archdeacon Basil Wilberforce, the Duke of Newcastle, the United States Ambassador, Lord Halifax, Dr. Ginsberg of the British Museum and Alice Buckton, Tudor Pole gave an account of the finding of the bowl and those present viewed it. Someone from this august gathering leaked the story to the Daily Express where it became front-page, 'Holy Grail Found,' sensationalist news. Goodchild had to write a letter to the paper

Above left: Archdeacon Wilberforce.
Above right: Tudor Pole's father, Thomas at the sluice.
Above: The Sapphire Blue Bowl.
Opposite: The Sapphire Blue Bowl with detail showing 8-petalled version of the Maltese Cross design.

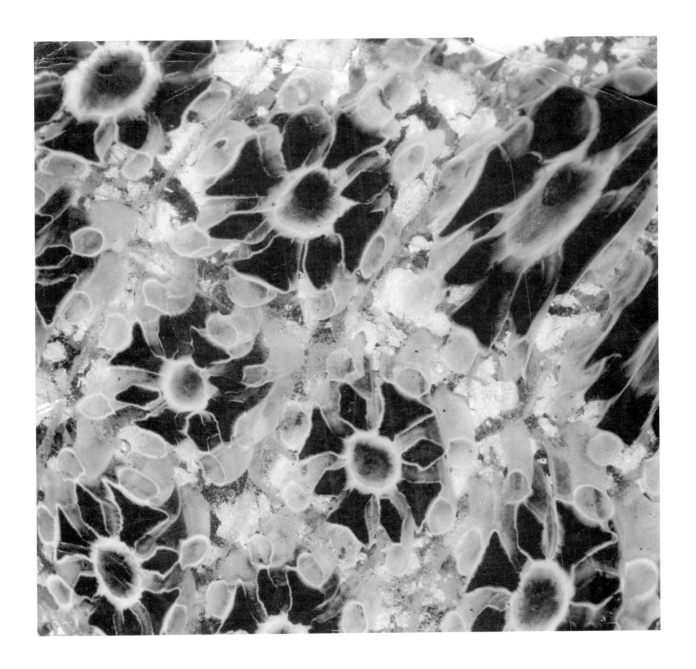

correcting many of the mistakes in the article and a three-day wonder faded away.

It was part of the vision of Tudor Pole that the bowl would play a part in the spiritual awakening of the coming era. The vessel itself seemed to indicate to the group in close contact with it, that is, WTP, Kitty and the Allen sisters, when it needed to travel. The first visit was to Iona, then an almost quietly forgotten island. WTP, the group and the bowl, now called variously the Cup of Peace or the Cup of Joy, touched and revived centres all over the island in preparation for its rebirth under the auspices of George MacLeod and the Iona Community. Subsequently WTP took the bowl to Palestine, Egypt, Syria, Constantinople, Mount Athos, Vienna, Budapest, Italy, France, Germany Holland and Rome. All these journeys happened between 1909 and the outbreak of war in 1914.

During both world wars the bowl was mainly in the care of Kitty Tudor Pole when it was withdrawn and 'quietly sleeping'. It travelled again between 1920 and 1935 mainly in the British Isles and was placed on the altars at Westminster Abbey and St. Paul's Cathedral. In his later life WTP considered keeping the bowl at the Hague to radiate world peace, but by December 1966 he decided to pass it into the care of the Chalice Well Trustees, "not as an object for veneration or as a precious relic to be worshipped, but as a symbol of unity, an insignia for the coming Aquarian age."

The Quest

It is interesting that in Fiona Macleod's Glastonbury triplet the last line says: "The Builders of Joy are the Children of Sorrow", for upon finding the bowl, WTP embarked upon a life long mission to try and find records and papers that would cast light on its links with the times of Jesus and the foundations of Christianity. This was a supreme effort which involved many expeditions to the Middle East and the chan-nelling of much material, which finally in his seventies came to nothing. He considered it the main failure of his life.

The background to this search, known as The Quest, was that the young

WTP could already 'see' the first World War looming and felt in his bones that if he could find parchments and records from the First Century substantiating the Cup of Peace then peace would indeed spread throughout the world. He left for Constantinople in August 1907 having already "visioned" the location of the lost library of the Emperor Justinian. This was where, he believed, that spiritual treasure was buried. WTP would gradually enlist all sorts of characters in The Quest including three Russian emigrés and Sir David Russell, his good friend and successful businessman who was based in Fife, Scotland. Russell had visited WTP in April 1912 to see the bowl and they had formed a close friendship which was to last a lifetime with almost daily contact, usually by letter. Over the following years Russell would financially support many of WTP's endeavours.

Early writings

As early as 1906 WTP had begun to publish his own writing – 'The Mind and its Mysteries' appeared in 'The Race Builder – official organ of The Thought Exchange' – an article about the development and control of thought power. This was followed by a 1909 leaflet 'Some Unrecognised Arguments in Favour of a Vegetarian Diet', a synopsis of an address he gave at Colston Hall Bristol. In 1916 Watkins printed 'The Spiritual Significance Of The Hour' with a forward by Lady Portsmouth and the book 'Christ in You' was published anonymously at this time. He also wrote for the Bahà'i newspaper 'Star of the West' during this period. He married Florence Snelling on 17th August 1912 who became his spiritual and life companion until her death in 1951.

As a visionary, WTP wrote in 'The Great War' (1915) that for seven years he had clearly watched a "conflict in the Air" approaching. He perceived this as a war between the powers of light and darkness:

'I have seen the great onrushing of the Breath of God descending nearer and nearer toward the ocean of the human mind. But as this great wave of consciousness approached humanity up rose from the human mind ocean the powers of selfishness, carnal-mindedness, fear and the rest – a great black host. All the powers standing for cruelty, injustice and militarism were marshalled in battle array, and the vision was an awful one!' (Private Dowding 1917).

With the work undertaken in Glastonbury, Iona and Constantinople, WTP was now gaining a maturity which allowed contact with higher spiritual forces. In the same piece of writing in 1915 WTP wrote: 'I believe I was intended to understand from this vision that the human race was approaching the greatest crisis in its history, and Humanity's dire need had drawn towards our realm the elder brothers of the race, that they might rescue us from the annihilation likely to result from a world conflagration.' Tudor Pole was about to step into this conflagration and play a hidden but powerful role in guiding humanity through the conflicts of 1914 – 1945.

The Silent Minute: Origins

In early December 1917, WTP was a British Officer fighting in the mountains around Jerusalem. On the eve of battle, he and another British Officer were discussing the war and its possible aftermath. Realising that his days on earth were to be shortened, the British Officer turned to TP and said "I shall not come through this struggle and, like millions of other men in this war, it will be my destiny to go on now. You (WTP) will survive and live to see a greater and more vital conflict fought out in every continent and ocean and in the air. When that time comes, remember us. We shall long to play our part wherever we may be. Give us the opportunity to do so, for that war for us will be a righteous war. We shall not fight with material weapons then, but we can help you if you will let us. We shall be an unseen but mighty army. Give us the chance to pull our weight. You will still have "time" available as your servant. Lend us a moment of it each day and through your Silence give us an opportunity. The power of Silence is greater than you know. When those tragic days arrive, do not forget us."

THE SILENT MINUTE

This Dedicated Minute is the period during which Big Ben strikes before the Nine O'clock News each evening. There is much to be gained by spending a short time in preparation for this Silence.

SUGGESTIONS FOR PREPARATION

Remember you are joining in a great Assembly now gathering before God as the seconds pass towards Nine O'clock. Of those still in this life some are suffering, some are sad ; many are lonely or fearful ; all are helped by your companionship in spirit.

Remember too those of the great company " which no man can number " whom for a little while we cannot see, but from whom there is no real separation.

" In quietness and in confidence " remember Christ is with you.
Lift up your heart in Thankfulness.
Then say, slowly, either our Lord's Prayer, or simply

" May Thy Will be done on earth—
Show me how to do my part."

DURING THE MINUTE

" Be still, and know that I am God."

Rest upon God's unchanging Love and Power.

Do not " think thoughts ";

Receive what God will give to you, and through you, to others. Never mind " how ? ", or whether you are " worthy ".

REST UPON GOD,

A card produced to promote The Silent Minute.

Next day the speaker was killed. WTP was severely wounded; stranded behind enemy lines he managed to get back to the British forces. It was then that the idea of a daily moment of united prayer and silence was born, becoming known as the Silent Minute, and eventually signalled by the chiming and striking of Big Ben at 9'o clock each evening.

The Silent Minute: Advent

The opportunity suggested in 1917 came during the evacuation from Dunkirk in the spring of 1940 when Britain stood unprotected and alone. Men and women of goodwill in Britain, the Commonwealth and elsewhere were asked to devote one minute of their time at nine each evening to pray for peace and to create a channel between the visible and the invisible worlds through which divine help and inspiration could be received. This dedicated minute had the support of H.M. King George VI, Prime Minister Winston Churchill and the Cabinet and many other leading figures in church and state. The minute was observed on land, sea and air, on the battlefields, in air raid shelters, hospitals and prison camps. It cut across all social boundaries.

The BBC, continuously lobbied by WTP and the Big Ben Council, decided to restore the voice of Big Ben (stopped because of the war) to broad-casting on Remembrance Sunday, November 10th 1940 as a signal for the Silent Minute each evening. The practice continued on the BBC Home Service until the mid 1950s. Its value was publicly recognised not only by President Roosevelt in America but also by the Nazi high command. Soon after the end of hostilities in Europe in 1945, a high ranking German Officer was quoted as saying, "During the war you had a secret weapon for which we could find no counter-measure and which we did not understand but it was very powerful. It was associated with the striking of Big Ben at nine each evening. I believed you called it 'The Silent Minute.'"

WTP was central to all this. He was busy setting up The Big Ben Inner Front (1941), the Silent Minute Fellowship (1943) and working to ensure the success of the venture. He wrote to David Russell after a meeting with Churchill:

"Up in the celestial regions it seemed numbers of radiant little angels carrying cornucopiae filled with myriads of mutli-coloured and flashing stars which they were emptying out into the dark firmament. From where, lines of light were being re-vitalised and spreading downwards toward the human worlds."

He encouraged the healer Harry Edwards to launch 'The Healing Minute' and emphasised the three keynotes of Remembrance (of those giving their lives for freedom), Thanksgiving (to the Creator) and Resolve (to unite in com-radeship for the building of a better world). "There is no power on earth that can withstand the united co-operation on spiritual levels of men and women of goodwill everywhere." WTP later wrote, "and it is for this reason that the continued observance of the Silent Minute is considered to be of such vital importance in the interest of human welfare." Currently Dorothy Forster continues to run the Silent Minute from London and Chalice Well encourages visitors to acknowledge a silent minute in the garden at noon and three in the afternoon.

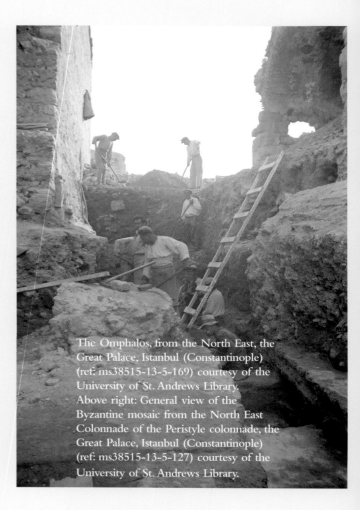

The Omphalos, from the North East, the Great Palace, Istanbul (Constantinople) (ref: ms38515-13-5-169) courtesy of the University of St. Andrews Library. Above right: General view of the Byzantine mosaic from the North East Colonnade of the Peristyle colonnade, the Great Palace, Istanbul (Constantinople) (ref: ms38515-13-5-127) courtesy of the University of St. Andrews Library.

Between the Wars

In the Birthday Honours List for 1919 Major Wellesley Tudor Pole was awarded the OBE for his war service. He set up his own business at 61 St. James Street, London; W Tudor Pole and Company, and expanded his horizons. Reading the copious correspondence between him and David Russell over these years one senses the real tension between the attempts

Opposite: Sir David Russell.

of WTP to be a businessman, earn money, support his family, and the pressures he felt from the spiritual worlds.

He was forever embarking on new business schemes often backed by David Russell, whether it was tea, clothing, bricks, concrete or trying to invent an "everlasting loaf" to help the world food shortage. He founded the Appeal for the Russian Clergy in 1926 and remained as treasurer until 1937. He and Florence now had three children and they were always on the move, living at many different addresses. Yet he was an intensely private man keeping his spiritual work separate from his business affairs and almost totally hidden from his family and the world until the later publication of pamphlets and books in the 1950s and 1960s.

There was the unfinished matter of The Quest, which he still believed would revive the consciousness of the world. Throughout the 1920s there were several attempts to reach the believed location of the papers and manuscripts but each time efforts were thwarted. It was small comfort to WTP to receive this channelled message in 1923: "We are aware of the difficulties by which you are surrounded and the apparent lack of clear guidance from our Sphere. Go forward cheerfully and in good fellowship." Other projects also took his time. In the late 1920s WTP was instrumental in introducing British capital into a major scheme of land reclamation and malaria control on the eastern seaboard of Italy. It was during this period that he met Padre Pio, the Catholic Saint, famous for his stigmata, as he later recounted in 'The Silent Road.'

The 1930s

WTP was aware that Iona had benefited from the earlier pilgrimage visits and he was keen to awaken or "bring on" the third point in a Glastonbury/Iona triangle, which was the Western Isle at Loch Erne. Avalon, Iona and the "the holy isle of the west" were the three great centres which Tudor Pole felt needed to be revitalised through pilgrimage and intentional prayer. In June 1930 he began to work with

Gertrude Mellor, "a woman of power" who would help him find his thus far missing holy isle in the west. He described her as of "immense physical proportions" with power and dignity and well steeped in working with the "cosmic centres" under "distinct commands." She had already carried out work with Glastonbury, Iona and Tintern.

They planned to visit Loch Erne on St. Michaels Day 1930 and WTP felt this would lead to a breakthrough in his work. At 12.45 he and Miss Mellor set off in a boat to the island (they used the name Eron although we today know it as Devenish). They both felt, according to WTP's subsequent letter to Russell describing the event that an age was closing and a new one was being born. "A great light seemed to shine down in countless rays upon Eron and from there to be thrown out over the world in all directions. At the same moment WTP became aware that the three principal centres of Avalon, Iona and Eron had become re-united and were re-consecrated for their holy mission in the New Time." They returned to the mainland at 4.00 p.m. Later WTP acknowledged to Russell that "it may take centuries for this fulfilment to manifest widely and leaven the thought of humanity."

During the rest of the decade WTP had brief but important contacts with Dion Fortune who was working out of Glastonbury, situating herself at the bottom of the Tor and working "for world welfare on special lines". She had sent WTP first drafts of her writing on healing, which he received favourably, calling Mrs. Firth (as he always referred to her) "the best magnetic healer of her generation". Meanwhile Alice Buckton was struggling to maintain her Chalice Well project and wrote to Russell and WTP asking for financial help. They advised her to apply to the Carnegie Foundation in America.

In 1934 WTP nearly died after suffering a serious illness. He wrote "I feel like an ancient worthy of this old planet just looking back again for a short visit". His wife Florence wrote to Russell: "No one knows what WTP has been through these last four years…. We have been quite isolated in Thames Ditton." Added to this was a general foreboding about the growing threat from Germany. He wrote: "At the moment I am a little overcome by the shadow cast by approaching events of a kind which is not simple to analyse." When the conflict came he was saddened by its inevitability. However he re-iterated to Russell: "There is not enough darkness in the whole world to extinguish the light of a single candle. Outer events in the end will be determined by the result of the inner conflict. We should never underestimate the potential value of effort, even by single individuals, in launching a worthwhile spiritual activity. This is a lesson everyone of us should learn and practise."

After the War

At the end of the war in 1945, having lost many of his papers when his office was bombed, WTP was in a philosophical mood when he wrote to his son Christopher from Luxor in Egypt: "I seem to have made rather a mess of my economic life and wonder what is important now and in the time on earth left to me?" He was sixty-one years old. He still believed that "to be alive and in incarnation just now both here and on the other side of what we call 'life' is an immense privilege and a very great responsibility."

There was the immediate danger of the use of newly invented nuclear weapons. With President Roosevelt's death their use was more likely. WTP drafted a statement of peaceful non-nuclear intent, and circulated it to politicians. He also carried out several correspondences on the spiritual implication of their use. He noted that conditions "between the worlds are unusually tense right now." He wrote to Russell just after the bombs had been dropped on Japan that "the origin of the atom is cosmic and to use it destructively as we have done is the final repudiation of the so called sanctity of the Hague Convention and all the agreements on weapons of war to which Britain and America have appended their signatures." However he was still hopeful believing that "the vast opportunities now available for the younger generations can only awaken to the fact that this Island can, if its people will, lead the world forward into the light."

Soon after the war WTP and his spiritual contemporary Ronald Heaver set up a company called Emion Ltd to research food, vitamins and alternative energy sources. A research laboratory was established in the basement at 22 Great Smith Street, Westminster and they appointed a young biochemist to carryout experiments on magnetism, electricity and ionisation. WTP was also carrying out his own research into pendulum dowsing for diagnosis in healing. He identified the malignant triad of illness as Worry, Anger and Fear!

The pioneers of the new age were now beginning to make their mark and WTP came into contact with many including Dr. Gordon Latto, Paul Brunton and Margaret Thornley. Cynthia Legh (later a Trustee at Chalice Well) was running the Big Ben office in London at this time. Occasionally he would spend time with his sister Kitty at Letchworth. At the end of 1947 he was feeling "mentally and bodily stranded" and spent several months staying with Margaret Thornley in Carbis Bay near St. Ives in Cornwall. Margaret was a mystic, a talented violinist, an artist, a Red Cross worker and President of the RSPCA. She carried out many pilgrimages on behalf of WTP, who she called her "wise friend". From this time would come the next stage of pilgrimage work through various St. Michael sites across Europe up into Cornwall, Devon and Somerset.

Margaret was inspired by her contact with WTP and recorded her journeys in tiny pictures drawn on a long ribbon scroll alongside the place names of each Michael site. The original satin ribbon was sent upon request to Queen Elizabeth the Queen Mother who had heard of the pilgrimages. The paper scroll passed to Cynthia Legh who conceived the idea of a prayer wheel for display. Oliver Morrel, one of the greatest furniture makers of the age, was brought in by the spiritual pioneer Sir George Trevelyan to make the wheel. At first it hung in Legh's sanctuary at Adlington and was then passed on to Chalice Well where it was set up in Little St. Michaels, "the most fitting home for it" according to Sir George.

As the 1950's progressed WTP became very concerned to find a cure for cancer. He stressed the importance of a diet of pure fresh fruit and juices without meat and controlled deep breathing in good air for the pure circulation of the blood. The metaphysical treatment he recommended included directed prayer and the spiritual realisation of wholeness through visualisation.

Detail of Prayer Wheel commemorating Margaret Thornley's pilgrimage.

Above: Front Cover of Wellesley Tudor Pole's book 'A Man Seen Afar'.

Later writing

From 1959 to 1968 WTP produced fourteen booklets and three books plus the further compilation of letters to Rosamond Lehmann 'My Dear Alexias'. These formed the main body of his written work in his lifetime. His first book 'The Silent Road – in the Light of Personal Experience' was published in 1960. It included chapters on 'Memory, Time and Precision', 'The Enigma of Sex', 'Spiritual Healing', 'The Mystery of Dreams' and 'The Lure of Ancient Egypt'. At the end of this book there was a short piece about the purchase of Chalice Well:

'At the beginning of 1959 it was my privilege to launch a wonderful adventure. The Chalice Well estate at Glastonbury Somerset lies on the slopes of Chalice Hill, almost under the shadow of the far-famed Michael Tor. For centuries past this hallowed site had been in private ownership, not easy of access to visitors and pilgrims.'

'With the co-operation of a group of friends, the property has now been vested in charitable trust and the hallowed well, the gardens and little St. Michael Hostel are now open to all comers, irrespective of race, class or creed.

I visited Glastonbury and Chalice Well for the first time in 1904 and at a time when the Chalice Well property belonged to a Catholic Order. I was allowed to visit the Well and to drink the healing and vitalising waters from its spring. I was left with a feeling of sanctity and inspiration, which has never left me. And I was left with something more, namely the premonition that in time to come I should be given the opportunity to come into possession of this truly wonderful place. Over half a century was to pass before the event fulfilled the premonition. Strange are the ways of Destiny!'

Tudor Pole went on to say on the final page of the book that he hoped Chalice Well would once more fulfil the inspiring mission of acting as a gateway through which revelation for coming times would flow. He closed with: "I firmly believe that it lies within the capacity of our children and their children to carry out this task."
During the 1960s Tudor Pole formed a friendship with the writer

Rosamond Lehmann and she helped him with his next book published in 1965, 'A Man Seen Afar.' This includes his visionary "Glimpses" of events at the time of Jesus, details of his understanding of the relationships between humanity and the nature kingdoms and a fascinating transcription of an interview between WTP and Rosamond Lehmann. A considerable correspondence took place between the two of them, extracts of which were later published in 1979. The book included tantalising details of his work "au dela" in the other worlds and details of some of his spiritual work at Chalice Well such as the creation of Arthur's Courtyard in the garden, and the Upper Room within Little St. Michael's.

In the last year of his life Walter Lang helped him to publish his final book 'Writing on the Ground' (1968). This work included his recollections of Abdu'l Baha, the leader of the Baha'i's, including his rescue by WTP during the First World War, and chapters on 'The Michael Tor', and 'The Closing Days of Atlantis'. It also included a forward by Sir David Russell who wrote: "His whole philosophy is a gentle, insistent assertion that the life we know is only a minute part of a greater continuum, existing far back and far ahead. Tudor Pole's ability to scan this continuum brings glimpses which are denied to most of us." There was also an insightful introduction by Walter Lang who wrote: "My own feeling is that TP's work is part, perhaps a small part, of a world wide operation at present being mounted by the higher powers. The work is to rewind the spiritual transformer of the planet in a different way, to prepare for a new flow of current from a solar source. How we do this rewinding at the present time will determine how the current will flow; and the manner of its flowing will determine the resonant frequency of humanity for the coming times."

In the last year of his life and racked by a painful cancer WTP continued to challenge humanity to rise to its fullest potential. New initiatives were still arising. When the BBC suddenly ceased broadcasting the chimes of Big Ben as a signal for The Silent Minute, WTP received inspiration, from the same high source as in 1940, that sound (silence) should be augmented by Light, and specifically that people should be invited to kindle and show permanently burning lights in their houses. These should preferably be of amber colour and burn in an upper room of the

Sir George Trevelyan and Cornwall Legh in the doorway of Little St. Michael's, on September 29th 1968 during a day of commemoration for W.T.P.

W.T.P
1968.

Portrait of WTP
by Kew Mills.

house. The lights, the source said, were an outward token of an inward purpose. This was the birth of the Lamplighter Movement, which WTP then asked Sir George Trevelyan to oversee. The movement was launched successfully; lamps are available today and there exist many testimonies of the deep joy and peace, which the lamps can bring into the keeper's house.

Tudor Pole passed over in September 1968. The next three issues of the Chalice Well magazine 'The Messenger' were full of moving tributes to this exceptional man.

What becomes clear from these is that despite his extraordinary life WTP came over as an ordinary man who was always good company. What Walter Lang called "the vast unordinariness of TP" was revealed only to a few people and only when he chose to.

In a book published in 1976 called 'Harvest of Light' Rosamond Lehmann paid the following tribute to WTP:
"He carried on a vast global correspondence throughout his adult life averaging over 100,000 words a year. His anger was reserved for prophets of doom, purveyors of doctrinaire theological systems and for all forms of authoritarian cant. Spiritual arrogance "sent shivers down his spine".
She concluded with one of WTP's main points:

"The Christos is not a person but a principle. A person, however Divine cannot be everywhere at once whereas a principle can. Available to be drawn on by everyone and by all forms life on every level of existence."

Towards the end of his life WTP believed that Glastonbury had a vital role to play in the world and he prayed that Chalice Well would blossom as part of that. One of the glowing tributes paid to him after his death described his breadth as "a gifted man, a mystic, a soldier, industrialist, author, student of archaeology, Founder of The Big Ben Silent Minute, and Founder and Chairman of the Chalice Well Trust."

The Story of the Trust: 'The Wonderful Adventure'

Pre 1959: Miss Buckton's Intentions

From the earliest days Alice Buckton had intended to turn the Chalice Well into a limited company. In the early successful years with good attendance at the summer school classes it seemed inevitable. By 1927 she was able to purchase Vine Cottage and St. Michael's Cottage to add to the estate. However, time passed, and the day-to-day running made it difficult for any legal formalisation to take place. Funds were always low and she struggled to pay the bills on time, often appealing to friends and associates for money. This created the situation in 1928 where she considered handing over the Chalice Well to the Churchman's Union. Plans were outlined for developing Chalice Well along conference centre lines, having a preparatory school in the three cottages and building a new girl's school on the site. When Annet Schepel died in early 1931 these plans seemed less likely than ever of coming to fruition. But there was movement that year when Articles of Association were drawn up and an appeal for £8,000 was launched. There was an impressive list of dignitaries in support of this, but somehow momentum was lost and nothing was finalised. What Alice referred to as 'the final step' was never taken.

So when Alice died in 1944 the Chalice Well was still being run in the same way as it was thirty-one years earlier when Alice and Annet had arrived from London. She had, however, made reference to the future of the estate in her will. This requested that a trust be formed and Ethel Edith Kenney and the Reverend George Seaver were named as the Trustees of a 'Chalice Well Trust.'

In her book about Alice, 'Beneath the Silent Tor', Tracy Cutting included a letter written just before Alice's death where she laid out her vision for the future of Chalice Well. It is worth re-printing here:

"It has long been the life of myself and my friends to serve this ancient property with its unique associations in a Trust. The names 'Isle of Avalon' and 'Chalice Well' are bywords in many lands today and all men and women of good will and of every nationality are welcomed here. Today

I must preserve this 'Mother Centre' so to speak, so that in all the days to be, men and women will find refreshment here in the cottages as well as in the monastic building which I took over from the Roman Catholic Fathers with their entire approval. I have already a well-advised group of friends knowing well my cherished plans. They will not only forthwith take over for me but will consider when and in what way the future working out of this charge may be influenced, so as to serve the needs of the coming time."

It was not to be, or not as she had imagined. Without her at the centre of things little progress was made and the properties which she had so diligently acquired were gradually sold off – the monastic building (Tor School), the cottages on Chilkwell Street, the fields, May Cottage, Vine Cottage and St. Michaels Cottage. For a time the vision faded so that when Dorothy Maclean, co-founder of the Findhorn Community in Scotland visited in the late 1940's she commented, "the Chalice Well itself was hard to find as it was covered with vegetation which we had to pull aside."

1958 Background to the Great Adventure

During 1958 events progressed. Tudor Pole was alerted to the fact that certain parts of the estate were coming onto the market and he was able to bring the importance of the site to the attention of the Big Ben Silent Minute network and apply their resources to the project. He had, after all, been waiting over half a century for this moment; a moment he probably believed was pre-destined.

Major Oliver G. Villiers D.S.O. who produced the 'Appreciation' pamphlet of WTP, also assembled a collection of his writing called 'Marching Forward' after WTP's death, which was never published. From this we can gain some insight into what lay behind what they called "the great adventure."

"Those who had the privilege of knowing Wellesley Tudor Pole realised that he came back into this world to accomplish a special mission for which he had been previously trained, and we now know how splen-

Above: Tudor Pole being interviewed by I.T.V.

didly he accomplished this work. ...I do not think it is an exaggeration to say that this spiritual and ancient ground was pre-ordained aeons and aeons ago by the Archangel Michael and the Elders, who must have known that it had a great purpose to fulfil through the many cycles of what we call time. Thus it has come about in recent years that a new spiritual factor has entered into the human consciousness of those prepared to receive it – it is referred to by T.P. as the Blended Ray. It was likewise necessary for this Ray to revitalise the kingdoms of this world and the elements, earth, fire, and water. In order to fulfil this purpose the Chalice Well Trust came into its own."

1959 – 1966 The Early Years of Restoration

The Trust documents were signed in London on 15th January 1959 at 34, Smith Square, SW1. Present were: Major Tudor Pole (in the Chair), A. Saville, Mrs Legh and L. Cornwall-Legh. In attendance were: Miss Hardcastle, Mrs Sandeman and J.M. Bowers. Apologies were received from: Miss Bright-Ashford and Clifford Wallis. The declaration was signed by all present and the conveyance of the Chalice Well property to the Trust was approved and signed. Mrs Sandeman (Christine Allen of former times) was appointed to be Clerk, Secretary and Custodian to the Trustees and Miss Hardcastle was appointed to supervise the gardens.

By the time of the second Trustee meeting in February, Mr W. Higgs had come on board and he and his wife were soon to become the first Wardens living in the re-named Little St. Michael's.

According to the memories of Felicity Hardcastle and Christine

Top: Original Trustee Group gather outside L.S.M. for a meeting.
Below: Original Warden Mrs. Higgs.

Sandeman, "the house was in bad repair, woodworm and death watch beetle wrought havoc, water oozed up through the old stone floors, no furniture, a garden full of weeds and the ground around the well overgrown and desolate. William Higgs worked throughout the early years for very little money and helped by 'his delightful wife' the garden flourished, lawns were made, flowers bloomed everywhere and it became a place of quiet, peace and beauty."

The first year concentrated on building and maintenance, launching Chalice Well publications, laying out the gardens, and pushing to extend the Companion supporter base. People gradually took on specific roles. Undoubtedly Tudor Pole was in a position of authority and was a strong guiding hand. When he was unable to attend a couple of Trustee meetings in 1964 things showed signs of wobbling and he soon returned to the tiller. Patrons were enlisted to help with various specific projects – locally there was Colonel Gould and Mr Scott Stokes of Glastonbury but also Mr Drummond of Drummond's Bank, London and WTP's old friend David Russell of Markinch, Fife.

Tudor Pole's life was still full of the remarkable. He recounted to Villiers the following:

"Having made my bid for the property I had agreed to pay the purchase price by a certain date. I also realised that at the moment I had not the money required but, at the same time, I knew that given sufficient time I would be able to raise the money required from friends. After careful thought I knew there was only one course open to me, and that was to go to my bank and ask for a loan to cover the entire amount required. I, therefore, went to my bank in the City and put my cards on the table to the Bank Manager, who was also a friend of mine. Naturally I told him that so soon as the deal had been completed I would bring him the title deeds, the value of which amply covered and more the purchase price, and it was my intention to form a Charity Trust so that the property would be preserved for all times."

T.P. with Trustee group.

Tudor Pole continued, but as was so often the case he referred to himself in the third person.

"The Manager agreed to advance the money required and T.P. left the bank. Just outside he met the President of the Bank who cheerfully enquired what he was doing there. T.P. told him the whole story and said how grateful he was for the kind way in which his request had been received, to which the President replied, 'Of course you got the loan, and if you hadn't, I would have gone in and jolly well given him the sack!"

Villiers says the reason for relating this financial transaction is that it clearly illustrates one of TP's remarkable facets. All who knew WTP realised that he always kept his word; 'his word was his bond' and that is precisely why he could make things happen.

The team he had assembled had many talents. Not least among these was Christine Sandeman. It was she who had been there in 1906 as part of the triad with Kitty Tudor Pole and her sister Janet. Life had taken her on quite a voyage, and she had married the Celtic visionary artist John Duncan who was associated with William Sharp and Dr. Goodchild. They had two daughters but the marriage was not to last. Christine insisted on leading her own life and joined the Women Police Volunteers in Edinburgh, which must have made for an interesting mix with her belief and work in Celtic mythology, St. Bride and Iona. By 1926 Christine had left her husband, and, on what seemed like a whim, took off for South Africa where she set up a welfare organisation providing nutritious food for the poor people of Cape Town. She married a Colonel Sandeman and returned to England several times, before basing herself at Chalice Well in 1959 to assist in establishing the Trust. She lived there through the early days in the spartan conditions of Little St. Michael's cottage.

Early days at the Well, 1960's, Christine Sandeman.

According to Patrick Benham's 'Avalonians' Christine had gone from Anglican to Christian Scientist and finally had become part of "a more obscure (probably 'esoteric') group," but she tended to keep her own counsel and was a deeply private person. Benham quoted from a letter written to the Glastonbury 'TORC' magazine from South Africa in 1972:

"I am so happy that the young are making some effort towards reviving a spiritual life in Glastonbury. I worked with W.T. Pole in the very beginning, collecting the money to buy Chalice Well and when it was bought was in charge. In those days we did so much: rebuilt the house; made a lovely garden; had lectures, interesting people staying – and then the excavation on the Tor. There was a resident Trustee (Higgs) and he was a marvel at planning things. The whole place began to come alive. I left after the last excavation, as it seemed better to have a man and wife in charge. (Mr and Mrs Higgs)."

The visitor's book from those early days indicates a panoply of esteemed guests who came to help anchor the vision. They included: Eric Hemery, Sir George Trevelyan, Isabel Hill Elder, the Prince of Saxe-Altenburg, the Bishop of Nagpur, Elizabeth Leader, Osman and Mary Caine, Ruth Bell, Naomi Edwards, Dorothy Maclean and Peter Caddy and of course Katharine Tudor Pole.

Felicity Hardcastle prepared the first booklet for sale to visitors. It was called 'A Short History' and gave details of the construction of the well.[1] It also included sections on 'the healing water', 'traditions', and 'romance', including the prophecy of Melkin which accentuated the stories and myths surrounding the Holy Grail. The Trust was described as "an instrument to acquire, preserve and safeguard for the public good in perpetuity the Chalice Well property as a place associated with Christian missionaries to these islands from the earliest times. The Chalice Well Spring, which comes from an unknown source, has been famed from ancient times for its healing properties and the water is available to all comers. The Trust relies on donations and a small income from its property to maintain the Chalice Well and surrounding Garden, and to provide for future development."

As early as 1964 there were indications of the impact of visitors on the gardens in this letter: "We have had to turn off the flow of water at the Lion's Head because the outlet pipe to the basin is stopped up. We have extracted from it a number of sweet or toffee papers and presumably there are more of these further down. As we ourselves do not indulge in these things, it suggests the younger generation!"

Chalice Well lid 1960.

1   note: see later extract "Construction of the Well"

During those early years the Trustee group would meet about four times a year sometimes in London, sometimes at Chalice Well, and liaise with Mr Higgs and Christine Sandeman on development projects. Included in these was the initial laying out of the gardens, sorting out the piping of the water through the gardens, a small library for the house, creating an entrance and approach to Little St. Michaels from Chilkwell Street and clearing and replanting the main orchard. There was a general appeal for money to friends in Britain, the Commonwealth and the U.S.A. and various ideas were put forward to extend the Companionship. Tudor Pole was also anxious to allow an archaeological dig on site, before the gardens were established, and Raleigh Radford of the Somerset Archaeological Society and Mr Dufty, Secretary of the Society of Antiquaries in London were enlisted. David Russell offered to pay for the research. In fact the Russell Trust provided many of the early funds for Chalice Well projects.

Tor School.

Early in 1961 the Tor School proposed building a swimming pool in the gardens for the boys. This was one of those inconvenient diversions that seemed to crop up over the years. The water for the pool was provided from the Chalice Well and it was built, used by the school, fell into disrepair and was eventually filled in. During 1962 the interior of Little St. Michaels was decorated and furnishings were donated so that three bedrooms could come into operation for guests. The charge was to be 17 shillings and sixpence (87 pence) per night for bed and breakfast and 5 shillings (25 pence) for an evening meal. The Custodian undertook catering. A big leap forward came later that year when a central heating system was installed.

At the end of July 1963 Tudor Pole brought forward plans for the renovation of Arthur's Courtyard area with a waterfall. Philip Rahtz was invited to Chalice Well to talk to the Trustees about future archaeological work. Rahtz had taken up a post at Birmingham University and he was sure the Department would back any work at Glastonbury. A series of digs were envisaged, the first being a four-week dig on the Tor under the auspices of the Chalice Well Trust Archaeological Committee.

After Christine Sandeman returned to South Africa in 1963, housekeepers came and went in swift succession and pressure seemed to build on the Higgs'. Michael Crichton was brought onto the Board in mid 1964 for his experience in financial matters.

Towards the end of 1965 the Glaston Tor School was put on the market, and Tudor Pole proposed "that all necessary steps be taken to obtain this property." This led to an interesting episode. Ronald Heaver an old associate and former treasurer and secretary to the Garden Tomb Association in Jerusalem also wanted to buy the school and set up the Glastonbury Foundation to do so. This group was concerned that a brewery was looking to purchase the property and they wanted to use the school as a spiritual and healing centre. Things were not easy between WTP and Heaver, and Peter Caddy from Findhorn became involved in the negoti-

ations. Eileen Caddy advised Peter that it was his task to bring the two men together but unfortunately he got caught in the crossfire. Heaver's group failed to find the money and Tudor Pole eventually secured the Tor School for the Chalice Well Trust. In the same sale the Trust also bought Vine and May Cottages. The school properties were immediately leased to Millfield School.

Around the time of the purchase of the Tor School Mr and Mrs Higgs retired, leaving the way open for new Custodians. By August 1966 John Simmons was the new Warden and Christine Sandeman returned as Custodian for a short spell. Mr and Mrs Simmons were to be paid £10

Excavations 1961.

Glaston Tor School advertisement.

a week and they remained as Wardens until Mr Simmons' death in 1979. The departure of the Higgs brought to a close the first phase of the Trust and opened the Simmons era, which was to last thirteen years.

1966-1979 Putting Down Roots

One of the first achievements under John Simmons was the establishment of 'The Chalice Well Messenger' a journal for Companions and supporters. Tudor Pole had suggested a Companion's journal as a way of strengthening links between Companions and to encourage greater support for the purpose of the Trust. Mr Kew Mills was appointed as editor and it was decided it would be the official publication of the Trust under the control of the Trustees.

Issue number one in Spring, 1967, featured a mix of articles and poetry and included a regular feature called 'The Warden's News' where Companions could be kept in touch with developments: "The most important single item," Simmons wrote, "planned to be finished by the end of March is the provision of an 'Upper Room' to provide a heart for Little St. Michael House. A sanctum sanctorum which has long been needed to replace the small sanctuary. It will run the whole length of the house with views of the Tor at one end and Wearyall Hill at the other." Over the next twelve years there were thirty-eight issues of 'The Messenger' produced under several editors.

Tudor Pole died in the autumn of 1968 and although there was great sorrow at his passing and many fulsome tributes were paid, the Simmons, John and Ida, and the Board of Trustees pushed forward with the project. Things were still small scale. 'The Messenger' began to feature articles on wider subjects such as 'Compassion in World Farming' and 'Fluoridation of water: modern menace to mankind'. The journal was now finding its way far and wide from Portugal, Switzerland and Morocco to Malaysia, Kenya and the United States.

Cornwall-Legh became Chairman of the Trust, a post he held for over twenty years, and Martin Israel and David Tudor Pole joined the Board.

The biggest challenge over the next few years was the clearance of the old school buildings from the lower part of the site. Millfield School had left and the buildings were in poor condition. There was an extended planning process involving the Secretary of State for the Environment. After a two-year delay, the land was cleared just before Christmas 1975, enabling a new entrance to be built and an opening up of this part of the garden. Visitor numbers in 1975 increased to over 5,000. The following year Dutch elm disease struck and Chalice Well lost all its thirty elm trees. Gifts of beech, mountain ash, oak and maple were received to fill the gaps. Despite the long hot summer, which resulted in the drought of 1976, the water from the spring continued to flow at its usual steady rate. The following year the new entrance wall was built and the gardens began to take on an appearance that would be more familiar to visitors today. The present bookshop was also built during this time and work on this whole area was formally dedicated and finished on June 2nd 1979.

Towards the end of the 1970's the tremendous strain of being Custodians at the Well began to increase. John wrote in 'The Messenger': "The passing years have seen many changes and we have on occasion been subjected to intense pressure of every kind to remove us from guardianship. But we have always found sufficient support to uphold us whenever needed." The Simmons had overseen what Sir George Trevelyan later called "a delaying period," a time of protection and the slow building up of energies. "The time," Sir George said, "was not yet right for forging ahead." But John's sudden death at Chalice Well in 1979 allowed a new era to begin as a young couple, Taras and Moya Kosikowsky, arrived and began work.

Top: Cornwall Legh.
Left: Castellated wall end of 1970's.
Little St. Michael's 1964.

1979-1986 A Flower Blossoms

Moya and Taras worked as volunteers in the garden and after a short break they became joint Custodians from March 1st 1980. There was a welcoming sense of joy and relief at the Trust. At Companions Day in the summer of 1980, Sir George Trevelyan spoke of "a flower that is now blossoming, a rose that is really opening." One of their first tasks was to remove a newly planted 'forest' of eighty-eight conifer trees that had been placed across the lower lawn after the dismantling of the school. They also began to build up the shop. Assisted particularly by Arthur and Pip Bourne, who had also become Trustees, they did much restorative work on the rest of the gardens which had suffered terribly in 1979 when flood-water redirected into the Chalice Well grounds, washed away many of the original paths and plants.

Taras (left) and Moya (right) with volunteers in the garden.

At the end of the 1970's the gardens had been temporarily closed and Taras and Moya were key to re-opening and restoring the site, which included much needed maintenance work on Little St. Michael's guesthouse and the Custodian's dwelling Vine Cottage. Regular meetings with Trustees were introduced. One of the early stalwarts Cynthia Legh stepped down and Tom Welch replaced Martin Israel. Pip and Arthur were the link on the ground with the Trustees. Sir George Trevelyan played an important role at this time, making frequent appearances at Companion's Day and offering support to Taras and Moya. He provided a vital link between Chalice Well and other emerging aspects of the new age in Britain.

Their son, Sean Michael, was born at Chalice Well on November 30th 1981 only two days after renovation work had been completed on the houses. They were soon made aware of the challenging nature of Chalice Well. "As you might imagine," wrote Taras in 1982, "so many seemingly

THE·PRAYER·OF·THE·CHALICE

Father, to Thee I raise my whole being,
—a vessel emptied of self. Accept, Lord,
this my emptiness, and so fill me with
Thyself—Thy Light, Thy Love, Thy
Life—that these Thy precious Gifts
may radiate through me and over=
flow the chalice of my heart into
the hearts of all with whom I
come in contact this day,
revealing unto them
the beauty of
Thy Joy
and
Wholeness
and
the
serenity
of Thy Peace
which nothing can destroy.

Prayer and calligraphy by Frances Nuttall

Top: Frances Nuttall.
Top right: Sir George Trevelyan 1981.
Right: Moya with 2 weeks old Sean above the Wellhead.
Above: Pippa Bourne 1980's.
Left: Frances Nuttall's 'The Prayer of the Chalice'.

'amazing ideas' show up on our doorstep brought by many well meaning individuals. Some of these ideas upon closer examination are in themselves fine, but within the greater context of Chalice Well do not feel right. The inner and outer balance is always at work."

Gradually Little St. Michael's was restored so that guests could stay on retreat again. There were now four bedrooms available with a minimum stay of three days and a maximum of two weeks. The cost was £8 a day. Long time supporter Frances Nuttall gave her 'Chalice Prayer Card' to the Trust to sell in the shop, and this is still available today. Tudor Pole's books and pamphlets were also sold in the shop and there was a reprint of four of his original booklets. Visitor numbers were now over 16,000 a year. The Chalice Well was drawing more and more people towards itself and there was an increasing sense of community.

By the summer of 1986 Taras and Moya had completed over six years of dedication and service, overseeing growth and expansion on every level. Companionship had grown from 153 to over 600 with visitor numbers up to 22,000 by the end of 1985. The Gatehouse Shop was paying its own way and was in profit. They had held the original vision of WTP while working successfully with his close friend Sir George Trevelyan and the chairman Cornwall-Legh. It was time to move on and so the Trust sought new Custodians.

1986–1995 Measured Success

It was now the turn of Leonard and Willa Sleath who came from Findhorn to take up the task. They were appointed by the Trustees as joint Wardens from 1st October 1986. They already had experience of living in community and had been on a spiritual journey which included Gurdjieff, Subud, the Guild of Pastoral Psychology, Findhorn and the ashram of Sathya Sai Baba. Along the way they had brought up a family of four children. At Findhorn Leonard had become a teacher of sacred dance and Willa was involved with the health of the community, the guest department and the Sanctuary. At Chalice Well, Willa took responsibility for the garden alongside a new gardener Pim de Grijff, the retreat house and the Upper Room, while Leonard dealt with administration, the properties and the bookshop. They followed the pattern of the previous Wardens producing one newsletter a year called 'The Chalice Well' producing numbers 10–19 between spring 1987 and spring 1996.

In their time at the Well Leonard and Willa oversaw forty-five improvement projects and witnessed quite a change on the Board of Trustees. When they arrived Antonia Yates and Cynthia Howles had joined and the link with the old esoteric order was still intact. As the project developed and became better known, the 'opening' that had started under Taras and Moya began to move quickly. By 1988 there were 31,000 visitors a year and over 800 Companions, which meant that full-time staff had to be employed. There were a succession of gardeners including Catherine Carter, Ian Sargeant and finally in this period Stephen George, who joined the team in November 1991. Frances Coxwell, who had worked with the previous Wardens, helped Leonard in the office and looked after the Companionship. However, there were still no paid cleaners or shop staff and Leonard and Willa carried out much of this work themselves, always aided by copious numbers of volunteers.

Leonard and Willa Sleath.

They began to spend money on upgrading the accommodation and work was carried out on Vine Cottage and Little St. Michael's including the building of a sauna room on the ground floor. There were the usual stresses and strains of being residential Wardens of a sacred site. During 1990 they had to introduce new guidelines for access and use of the Upper Room, there was a spate of burglaries to the shop, and Leonard could often be found patrolling the gardens at night, lovingly ejecting any unwelcome visitor! When they needed a break Arthur and Pip Bourne were still around to take over as relief Wardens. Arthur died towards the end of 1988 and Cynthia Howles paid tribute to his dedicated service to the Well: "his spirit will be indelibly impressed upon both the gardens and the Trust, because he was never a man to flinch from working with his hands as well as with his heart and mind."

Leonard and Willa always had an international focus and after visiting Russia in 1988 they welcomed Russian visitors to stay at the Well. In the garden there were two big changes. The first was the conversion of an old open barn at the bottom of the garden into a gardener's centre to house tools and equipment. This building would also double as a tea and coffee bar on Companion's Day and other special occasions. Secondly, John Wilkes from Emerson College in Sussex was employed to create a water feature known as a flowform, which would direct water into the

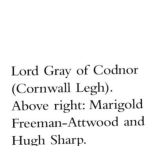

Lord Gray of Codnor
(Cornwall Legh).
Above right: Marigold
Freeman-Attwood and
Hugh Sharp.

Vesica Pool. The flowform was later found to enhance the subtle qualities of the water, and was completed in March 1993.

In 1989 Chalice Well Chairman Cornwall-Legh finally became Lord Grey of Codnor (pronounced Cudra), a process that had taken 493 years to resolve. He commented, "the Queen was advised to revive the title, which she has done. The hearing lasted for two days, and I'm so damn deaf I couldn't hear half of it, but we finally got there." He didn't intend to go to the House often because of his age, but revealingly commented, "if something comes up – like the scandalous fluoridisation issue – then I'll make the trip. Ermine robes? No need for all that funny stuff. If I go it will be in a suit and tie." This gives us a glimpse of the man who held the Chair from the days of Tudor Pole through into the 1990's.

As Lord Grey passed his 90th birthday in 1993 he decided to step down and Roy Procter, who had become a trustee in 1991, became the new Chairman. Again the ever-changing currents that flow through Chalice Well were moving things along. Cynthia Howles and Marigold Freeman-Attwood stepped down and Martin Oliver, retired Warden of Abbey House in Glastonbury, and business consultant Barry Taylor were added to the Board. A review of all aspects of the activities at Chalice Well was carried out and Leonard and Willa, who had now passed retirement age began to think about stepping down.

They had overseen nine years of gradual development and the time had come to leave. Leonard wrote, "In its philosophy Chalice Well is universal, embracing all genuine faiths and helping to remove the barriers between them. It fosters spiritual growth and spiritual fulfilment by being open-hearted, open-minded, very clear and very tolerant. We hope it will always remain thus and be a source of inspiration." Willa wrote, "It has been very rewarding, meeting people in the garden and the Retreat House. Strange is the path of love, which has nourished me in the flowing of our time here. Perhaps we shall meet with our back to an ancient yew and the sound of running water, or just to browse." To this day, Willa remains a volunteer in the Gatehouse.

Roy Procter.

Fred and Colleen Rosado.
Top: Fred and Colleen with
the 'team'.

1996–1998 A Time of Great Change

From this point the changes came thick and fast. The visitor numbers and the Companionship had grown to a level where 'transformation' was knocking at the door. John Rowntree and Ann Procter had joined the Board and the new incumbents, now called 'Resident Guardians' were to be Joseph 'Fred' and Colleen Rosado from Long Island, New York. Their background was in healing, running courses and spiritual questing tours and trading in herbal remedies. They were selected from a wide variety of applicants and felt they were destined to come and serve the Well, "by a strange surge of knowing." Colleen had visited Glastonbury and Chalice Well before and together with Fred they felt they could create a sense of community between Chalice Well and the town and establish a children's garden, which would be family orientated.

It was another new beginning for the great adventure. Fred and Colleen with the Trustees oversaw the creation of a completely new entrance to the gardens, with the old tarmac in front of the cottages removed and a cobbled pathway passing under a pergola leading up to a gatehouse. This was made possible by a generous legacy from Companion Alice Twydell. Gardener Stephen George reported how Michael Eisele and he spent more time with builder's trowels in their hands than with gardening tools. Martin Faulkner did much of the building work and their skills as stone workers were tested and honed. Work included a curved stone seat built into Arthur's Courtyard and a rough stone path built to open up the meadow so that there was now an 'outer' sanctuary with magnificent views over the vale. There was new crazy paving of solid grey lias stone laid around the vesica pool and a new stone angel carved by Michael Eisele to replace the one stolen five years previously.

A new team assembled around Fred and Colleen, which included Dennis Morris, Alan Royce, Diana Griffiths and Marie Tilley. As visitor numbers to Little St. Michael's rose rapidly Marie took on a housekeeper role. After the garage was converted to office space Alan began to look into the mountains of paper and archive material which had never been sorted since the first days of the Trust. This led to the setting up of the Chalice Well Archive under the stewardship of Dr Tim Hopkinson-Ball and later Paul Fletcher. Alan Levett became Registrar of Companions. With the gardeners there was now a team of eight people.

One of Tudor Pole's original visions was for a meeting room where workshops, talks and classes could be held. John Rowntree gifted enough money for this to go ahead and plans were drawn up for a large room to be added to the 'Tor end' of the cottages. Trustee Barry Taylor formalised the financial management of the charity and began to produce a set of budgets enabling Trustees to monitor the finances more easily. Computers were upgraded and the office became more business-like. Gradually the old guard were passing away and leaving – Antonia Yates and Pip Bourne had stepped down. Moya Kosikowsky, Dr Philip Jackson and Serena Roney-Dougal joined the Board, increasing local representation. Under Fred and Colleen the annual 'Chalice Well' magazine transformed itself into the full colour and larger size 'Messenger' edited

by Martin Oliver. By its second issue in February 1999 Roy Procter was writing, "It has been an eventful year! As many of you will know, our Resident Guardians, Colleen and Fred Rosado, have decided that it was time to move on." The Rosados had provided new impetus, real transformational American energy and shortly before leaving wrote: "This is a time of deep significance, not only for the human race, but for life in every form upon earth. There is a sweeping inner revolution taking place. Everywhere there is a deep thirst for spiritual connection. Of the many seekers we watch pass through the gateway of Chalice Well, there is intense interest in various forms of exploration and spiritual practice."

The challenge now for the Chalice Well was to be open and universal to the increasing number of visitors and pilgrims while retaining the keynotes of the Trust. "To attempt a stretch between heaven and earth," said the 'Messenger' of 1999, "to honour all that the Chalice Well means in further dimensions of awareness, while at the same time keeping our feet on the ground."

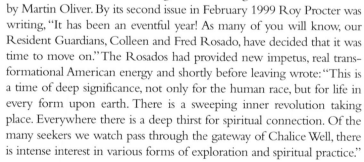

Entrance to Chalice Well.

Guardians Lynne and
Michael Orchard.
Below: Trustee Mary Priest-
Cobern.

1998-2005 A Further Expansion

Michael and Lynne Orchard had been interviewed for the Guardians post in 1995 but they were about to go abroad and withdrew. Their application letter lay hidden for nearly three years before surfacing as the post became vacant again. It was a unanimous decision to appoint them. Their background was in healing and holistic training in aromatherapy, massage, anatomy and physiology. They had previously run a centre in Exeter and had been visiting Chalice Well since 1986. Michael had lived in Glastonbury between 1975-1982, helping the late Arabella Churchill to establish the Children's World charity.

They entered quietly, listening to the spirit of the place. By Spring 2000 the newsletter became the A4 size 'Chalice', and there was an increase in day-to-day activities at the Well with events in the garden and celebrations organised by the Trust to mark the festivals at the equinoxes and solstices as well as the cross-quarter days.

Change continued to take place as Stephen George moved on from Head Gardener and Ark Redwood arrived. Paths were laid up into the Meadow and a Picnic Area was developed, thus taking pressure off the main gardens on busy summer days. A new arrival on the Trustee Board was Mary Priest-Cobern. The Chalice Well team now included Nikki MacBeth, Helen Drever, Kelvin McNulty and Jacqui Percy, some of whom had worked with the Rosados. The office was expanded and Chalice Well moved into the twenty-first century with a database, Internet access and email. The website was launched on November 1st 2000. A new guidebook updating the old 'blue book' of Felicity Hardcastle from the early 1960's was assembled by Trustee Ann Procter. There was a feeling of momentum in the air: "There is so much life, vitality and abundance at Chalice Well at the moment.' However, in the same issue of 'The Chalice' Roy Procter wrote that "financial considerations loom large." With the increased level of activity the wages bill was rising and there needed to be adequate income and detailed budget monitoring. It was a balancing act, which would occupy Michael and Lynne through their years as Guardians.

As they went into 2001 the Guardians outlined three key areas of interest that they wanted to explore. Firstly, ways of 'freeing' the water, secondly creating new 'sacred space' in the garden and thirdly opening up the Well to all who wished to play a part in its future. At this time Alan Gloak, Sig Lonegren and Kyrin Singleton joined the Trustees. The staff team began to change and in came Simon and Natasha Wardle and Nicholas Mann. A new kitchen was put into Little St. Michael's and an archive room was established.

By the end of 2001 a core group of about forty-five people (Trustees, staff and volunteers) were involved on a regular basis with the running of the Well. There were now over 2000 companions. During 2002 the Trust bought the end of terrace house adjoining the gardens in Chilkwell Street. Chalice Well Lodge provided extra accommodation and allowed for longer stays. Celebrating their fourth year as Guardians Michael and Lynne wrote, "some days the chaos is in the ascendant; computers and phones malfunction, kids run wild in the gardens, people get uptight or impatient. At other times an extraordinary peace can envelop the place and one can feel as if wrapped in Angel's wings, and everything is full of light and radiance. Our work here, with everyone in the team, is to hold the space, to keep the balance."

Over the next couple of years Michael and Lynne introduced other innovations including a new sanctuary space near the Well head, which discovered new springs. As part of their wish to open up the waters a rill was built winding across the lower lawn. The well lid was restored by Hamish Miller and events such as regular full-moon evenings in the summer months, a mid-summer concert, an Angel and Nature Spirits day and a healing weekend were successfully introduced. Alan Gloak became chairman during this time. In response to the events of 9/11 they introduced a weekly evening meditation in the Upper Room for Companions and their guests.

By early 2005 many Companions and the Trustees felt there was need for a pause in the pace of change and a two-year period of quiet was agreed upon. There was to be a time of stillness and reflection to let the energies settle. Kyrin Singleton became the new Chair while Tyna Redpath and Joanna Laxton joined the board. However things were not to remain quiet for very long; in quick succession Michael and Lynne resigned and Kyrin stepped down due to ill health. Roy Procter returned to jointly Chair the Trust with Tyna for a one-year term. It was all change at the Well once more.

2005 – 2008 New Pathways

In one of the biggest changes in the Trust's history it was decided not to appoint new resident Guardians but to explore a different way of running the Trust. This would necessitate a more devolved structure including a coordinator/manager, a staff circle, much more involvement from the Trustees, and an exploration of how to maintain Chalice Well as a 'living sanctuary' in the new century. For one year Chris Marshall became co-ordinator and was followed by Natasha Wardle as Manager. At Companion's Day 2006 Roy Procter stepped down after fifteen years of service and Joanna Laxton joined Tyna to jointly chair the Trust. The aim was towards greater participation. Tyna wrote in the Chalice, "in order to move forward and meet the challenges of being a 21st century organisation we need to create a structure, within the remit of our charitable status, where communication is creative, transparent, open and free flowing between our various groupings." Sophie Knock replaced Sig Lonegren on the trustee board. In the garden health and safety issues were addressed and Little St. Michael's finally received a new and insulated roof. Ann Procter edited and compiled the first book about Chalice Well, 'This Enchanting Place – Facets of Chalice Well' which included fascinating contributions from many different sources. From issue 17 'The Chalice' returned to its original A5 size and continued under the editorship of the Chalice Well archivist Paul Fletcher.

Alongside the understanding of Chalice Well as a 'living sanctuary,' the

From above left: Co-chairs, Jo Laxton and Tyna Redpath and Trustee Sophie Knock.

concept of 'living intention' was introduced as a keynote. "The phrase living intention implies 'life with purpose,' Trustee Joanna Laxton wrote in 'The Chalice.' "Intentional living requires inner preparation through reflection on the purpose and activities of each day (and/or longer term plans) and an attitude of constant recollection to maintain that focus. It means being fully 'present,' and operating from a calm inspirational centre where mind and emotions are stilled and head and heart are united in deep purpose. This is the place where spiritual energy is found."

Today with all the challenges of the modern world it seems more important than ever that a haven like Chalice Well should exist. The story manifesting here is a fascinating example of co-operation between different spiritual paths, between humanity and nature, and of caring stewardship for one of the most ancient wells in the world.

View of the Rill running across the lower gardens.

In the Gardens

A walk through the garden landscape

The Trust protects an area of some 12 acres (5 hectares) and this comprises both public & private gardens.

The Chalice Well and the main gardens are enfolded in the vale between Chalice Hill and the Tor and the garden's landscape (or aspect) naturally rises upward from the bottom of the garden toward the Well head at the top. The gardens progress from the open space of the lower lawns following the course of the waters to their source. It is a garden of many 'rooms' each with different qualities, features and planting, but all combine to create a living sanctuary of healing, sanctity and peace.

A pair of wrought iron gates fashioned in the form of the Vesica Piscis open to welcome the visitor up the pergola path adjacent to Little St. Michael's Retreat House and towards the garden. In summer the pergola drips with the fragrant fronds of the White Wisteria, climbing roses and an abundance of hanging baskets. Growing against the wall of Little St Michael's are a number of well-established shrubs, including *Garrya elliptica*, a winter-flowering honeysuckle *(Lonicera fragrantissima)*.

The vesica, symbol of the union and dissolution of polarities can be seen throughout the gardens in many forms. There is a vesica fashioned from quartz and amethyst set in the cobbled path over which the visitor walks before passing through a second vesica gate adjacent to the Gatehouse.

Behind the Gatehouse is a 100ft bed, consisting of a number of established shrubs including: a Tree Peony *(Paeonia delavayi var. 'lutea')*, a Smoke Bush

(Cotinus coggygria) whose fronds after a light shower look like chandeliers, Jerusalem Sage *(Phlomis fruticosa)*, *Viburnum x burkwoodii*, *Cistus x cyprius*, a cotoneaster and the lovely *Daphne odora* 'Aureomarginata', whose intoxicating perfume graces the air in early spring.

At the foot of the garden lies the Vesica Pool; so called because within its design are contained two perfect interlocking circles. On a sunny day its surface allows the sparkling play of sunlight on water and fed from water cascading through a flow form, is the perfect spot to sit and hear the mel-lifluous sounds of tumbling water.

John Wilke's seven bowled flowform was installed in 1993 and replaced the existing open shuted waterfall. In each of the bowls the water describes a perfect figure of eight. If the flow of the waters circulation in the third and eighth bowl are timed and counted, it can be observed that they circulate at 18 and 72 times per minute. These are the rates of the breath and the heartbeat. The flowform is set in a rockery with a few dwarf conifers mostly cedar, cypress and juniper, giving some evergreen structure. Other evergreens include hebe, santolina, box, and heather. Perennials include Pasque Flower *(Pulsatilla vulgaris)*, Angels' Fishing Rods *(Dierama spp.)*, Digitalis, Alchemilla, Osteospermum, Hardy Geraniums, Polygonum, Bugle *(Ajuga reptans)*, and Red Valerian *(Kentranthus rubber)* and in summer months the flowform is framed with white Calla Lilies and Blue Irises.

The most recent addition to the gardens, is the rill which runs from the vesica pool and takes the waters out of the gardens. Leaking Victorian clay pipework led to regular flooding of the lower lawns and a decision was taken to allow the waters to flow above ground.

Beside the Vesica Pool grows one of the garden's three Holy Thorn Trees. The Holy Thorn is woven into Glastonbury lore and is said to be testament to the visit of Joseph of Arimathea after the crucifixion. Legends claim that he landed on Wearyall Hill, thrust his staff into the ground and it took root and flowered. The botanical name of the plant is *Cretaegnus monogyna* and is not native to British soil. It is more usually found growing in the Middle East where it is used by shepherds to make walking sticks. It is a difficult tree to propagate as the thorn has to be

Flowform with Calla Lilies.

grafted onto a Hawthorn rootstock. The biennial flowering, coinciding with Easter & Christmas, of white flower blossom among scarlet berries is a source of wonder to many.

Above the Vesica Pool stand two tall yew trees of large girth but indeterminate age. Many consider these to be guardians of the entrance to the "inner garden paths". The Yew is significant in ancient lore and is associated with Ygdrassil or the World Tree. Yews are often planted in churchyards and sacred sites. There are many Yew trees growing in the Chalice Well Garden, most provide a quiet and endarkened canopy under which to contemplate and go within. It can be guessed that perhaps the yew tree had some significance in this locale in times past, an upturned and perfectly preserved stump being found during excavations in the Well shaft in the early 1960's

Through the guardian Yew Trees is glimpsed an open wooden door which leads into "Arthur's Courtyard" and the healing pool. To its right, is a gate leading to Wellhouse Lane and the neighbouring White Spring. Known as the "Monk's Gate", this is the entrance through which TP first came into the gardens in 1904 as a young man. Adjacent, is a yew tree whose trunk has curiously split in two and then rejoined, creating a natural vesica form which many believe to be a representation of the Divine Feminine.

Main picture: The Guardian Yews.
Inset: The Vesica Yew.

The branches of this tree are often found hanging with ribbons and "tree favours", an ancient tradition with which prayers and blessings are asked, offered and taken on the wind to their destination.

It was WTP who named "Arthur's Courtyard" and it houses the foundations of the original 'spa' baths which were erected in the late 1700's. Photographs taken in the early part of the 20th Century show a building and covered walkway, into which the pilgrims would have entered to "take the waters". The walled Courtyard is shaded by the canopy of a large Yew Tree under which grow ivy, woodland ferns and shade-loving plants. The shallow pool is fed from a rill and vivid red waterfall at the foot of which is the supposed spot where the Michael and Mary Ley (or earth energy) lines converge.

The large bush in the centre is an *Elaeagnus x ebbingei*, which communicated its presence to the Head Gardener, who responded by giving it all due acknowledgement and appreciation and carefully tending and shaping its form in order that it should thrive and flourish.

The plants in pots behind the healing pool are tree ferns *(Dicksonia antarctica)*, which are not entirely hardy, and require their heads to be wrapped during the winter months. The two gold-flecked evergreen shrubs behind the stone seat are Spotted Laurels *(Aucuba japonica)*, which are useful plants because they are amongst the few which will thrive in deep shade. The bank at the back is actually very wet, being one of the few places where water from the neighbouring 'White Spring' enters the garden. Evidence of this can be ascertained by peering behind the stone seat, and observing the calcification seeping down the bank from where the waterfall cascades. The bed at the bottom of the steps is also very wet, and so is planted with suitable plants such as the pendulous Sedge and the lovely Calla Lily *(Zantedeschia aethiopica)*, with its pure white flowers lighting up the shade.

On either side of the doorway into the court stand two large ammonite fossils. Ammonites are frequently unearthed in the gardens and confirm that the land, in prehistoric times was once submerged. Many of those found have been set into the walls and pathways and can be glimpsed in the surround of the Well head itself. These two larger examples however, were not found in the Gardens but were graciously given into the Trust's care by St. Benedict's Church in Glastonbury.

A flight of steps lead out of Arthur's Court and up onto the main path to the Well itself. The path, as with many of the garden's paths is made of blue lias stone mined in the surrounding Mendip Hills. Above the wall are planted a grove of Hazels, deliciously-scented *Viburnum farreri*, and the Wintersweet *(Chimonanthus praecox)*, a secluded spot in which to sit unnoticed and listen to the sounds of the cascading waterfall.

Opposite and to the right is a wooden shelter in which to take refuge on rainy days. Adjacent is a venerable Bay tree beside more steps leading to an upper bank. The bank is home to a number of trees including a magnificent Silver Birch, which is known affectionately as 'Grandmother Birch', because many believe her to be a wise being with much to teach.

The Lion's Head drinking fountain which is piped directly from the source of the Well sits in a sunken garden with formal lawns and trimmed box hedging. The Lion has become bearded with iron ore and glasses are left standing under the fount, upon two millstones, inviting refreshment. Above the Lion's head stands a smaller Holy Thorn Tree and further verdant lawns surrounded by vibrant and colourful flower beds.

In the midst of the flowers sits the Angel seat in a bower of fragrant Honeysuckle, wild 'Albertine', rose and a *Clematis Montana* which grow in the Garden's largest flower beds. Flowers are frequently placed in her hands. This is another lovely spot in which to catch the warmth of the sun as it rises over the Tor.

The beds are planted with a year round spectacular of colour and form with recognisable favourites, including: Delphiniums, Hollyhocks, Dahlias, Calendula, Violas, Nicotiana, Hardy Geraniums, Bells of Ireland, and Mignonette.

Shrubs include:- the fine smelling shrub rose, *Rosa* 'Blanc De Coubert', situated either side of the beginning of the pathway and on the left side; Camellias, Pieris, Photinia, Cercis, a yellow-berried Cotoneaster, orange-flowering *Colutea arborescens*, Weigela, Hamamelis (Witch-Hazel), Lilac, Ceanothus, the Beauty Berry *(Callicarpa bodinieri var, giraldii* 'Profusion')*, three of which are situated in front of a *Buddleia alternifolia*, and on the right, Cotoneaster, Euonymus, Berberis, the wonderful cream-tassel flowered *Itea ilicifolia*, Spiraea, Physocarpus, Mahonia, a tall *Prunus* 'Pandora', and next to it, *Daphne tangutica*, Syringa, *Rosa* 'White Cloud' and a Clematis 'Madame Le Grange' next to the gate.

Clockwise from top right: Datura and Mother and Child Sculpture; Allium; Aquilegia; Aquilegia.

Through the wrought iron gate one enters the Well head and surrounding sanctuary. Two further Yew trees stand as sentinels above the Well itself and beneath them a Bay Laurel in whose branches are hung the hopes and prayers of visitors or pilgrims. The well is encircled by a stone wall seat which allows those who come to sit in quiet repose and contemplation.

Varieties of ferns with their calming green palate and subtle planting of Lily-of-the-Valley, Dog's Tooth Violet, Welsh Poppy, Violas, Cyclamen Hostas and Hellebores assist the contemplative process. In early spring Snowdrops and a beautiful *Magnolia stellata* speak promise of the gathering light.

In 2003 the area surrounding the Well was re-landscaped. During the renovation of the retaining walls, further springs of water were discovered. The flow of the springs is slight but constant and the waters are of a different mineral composition than the water of the Well.

By a synchronicity, the garden was visited by Ganesh, an Indian stone carver who gifted a statue of a mother and child, copied after an Eric Gill original. This was placed in an alcove of the retaining wall and sits above the new-found spring.

The Meadow

The Meadow, above the main gardens is entered through the Beech hedge and a Willow arch which is training espalier apple trees ('Laxton's Superb'), to form a living archway. This meadow was re-landscaped at the end of 1999. It had been opened to the public, after having been separated from the rest of the hillside, a few years before, and people had been (and still are) encouraged to have their picnics here instead of in the rest of the garden. Trees were planted along the periphery, including Ash, Poplar, Silver Birch, Rowan and Alder, and later a Weeping Mulberry and a swing seat put in place offering views of the Tor. The adjacent wooden peace pole was made and donated by John Appleton of The Peace Pole Project, and carries the words "May Peace Prevail on Earth" in four different languages, English, Japanese, Latin and the ancient Runic Script.

Inset: View of the Tor
from the Meadow.
Main pic: Cress field.

Buckton's Orchard.
Inset: Anthony Ward,
Orchard Keeper harvesting
the apple crop.

Four Fields: The Orchards of the Chalice Well Gardens

To the North, South, East and West of the Gardens are the four fields owned by the Trust which protect the Well from unsympathetic development and in recent years have, with the exception of the Cress Field, been replanted and managed as orchards. These fields are rarely open to the public gaze and are kept for nature, the elementals and biodiversity with limited human impact.

The main orchard named Buckton's Orchard after Alice Buckton, is at the back of Little St Michaels on the slopes of Chalice Hill to the north overlooking the Gardens. More than a decade ago new planting began here under previous Head Gardener Stephen George with help from Major Ian Rands and the Glastonbury Conservation Society tree planting team in a remnant orchard of old apple trees covered in mistletoe.

Today there are 103 young standard fruit trees in Buckton's – 96 of which are dessert apple varieties, 5 are pears, and 2 are plums. There are 19 varieties of traditional English apples in the orchard - all supplied by John Dennis from Top Fruit Trees in North Cadbury - with Ashmeads Kernel, James Grieve, Laxtons Superb, Ribston Pippin, Blenheim Orange, and Crispin particularly well-represented. 7 venerable old apple trees remain from earlier plantings at least 50+ years ago and there is even the living husk of a hollowed-out pear tree in the middle of the orchard.

Above the orchard is a fenced shelter-belt of young trees acting as a wildlife and nature corridor and buffer zone between Bucktons and Clifford Gould's land on Chalice Hill. This belt continues above the Cress Field and is home to a variety of wildlife mammals.

In 2002 local beekeeper Andrew Groves was invited to set up two hives to improve pollination in the orchard. His successor, Tom Done from Butleigh, manages these hives today and his honey is sold in the shop. The original intention was not simply to restore the ancient orchard but eventually to have enough fruit to produce Chalice Well apple juice. In

2006 this goal was finally achieved when Hecks of Street turned six boxes of apples hand picked by staff into 77 bottles of apple juice for sale in the Chalice Well shop. In 2007 the apple harvest was even better and 183 bottles of juice were produced for sale or use in seasonal ceremonies and celebrations.

Grassland management in Buckton's Orchard was for many years based on sheep pasture but after extensive damage to trees in summer 2007 from sheep stripping bark above the wire mesh protectors, The Trust is currently experimenting with sheep free grass management and the promotion of wildlife and biodiversity. However local shepherd, Nigel Paul from Common Moor Farm in Glastonbury, still pastures his sheep around the other three fields – The Cress Field; The Tor Orchard and the Plum Orchard.

The Cress Field to the East is not strictly an orchard but has a handful of very ancient apple trees and one young apple tree donated by the Tudor Pole family in memory of David Tudor Pole. On the higher slopes are a handful of recently planted ornamental trees including Cherry, Horse Chestnut, Oak and Spindle. In times past, this field supported a rectangular watercress bed fed from another spring that now only flows intermittently.

The Tor Orchard to the South on the corner of Well House Lane and Coursing Batch is a new apple orchard of 26 young standard apples planted in March 2005 to celebrate local Somerset varieties such as Tom Putt, Hoary Morning and Court de Wyck (although Red Bramley and Falstaff come from outside the county) and in 5-10 years it too will hopefully be producing fruit to press for Chalice Well apple juice.

The Plum Orchard to the West, surrounded by houses on the other side of Chilkwell Street, was the last orchard to be cleared, re-fenced and have a new mixed native hedge planted on its north side. 2008 saw the planting of five new standard plum trees – 3 Victorias and 2 Dennistons Superb Imperial Gage – to add to the mixture of plums, cherries and apples already present (there is even a fig in the top right hand corner of the orchard).

The management of the Orchard land is chemical free in line with the conservation ethos of the Trust.

Planting and Gardening Philosophy

Whilst in the Garden, many talk of a heightening of sensory acuity; colours, light, fragrance and sound all serve to create an intensity. Creating a sensory world with opportunities for experience and relationship underlies the planting philosophy. The choosing of plants is subject not only to the process of intuition but also to the consideration that form, colour and aroma invite the beholder to encounter and connect.

It is a garden that must allow and support the mystical experience and so the relationship with nature and the nature kingdoms must be a conscious and harmonious one.

Since 2000 the garden has been organic, and in recent years has become completely peat-free with regard to bought-in proprietary composts. Although weeds are obviously controlled, there are areas where they are tolerated. Every year the soil is mulched, where appropriate, either with leaf mould or compost thus avoiding complications associated with the

practice of digging. The soil is viewed as a living organism in itself, comprising a myriad of creatures and minerals existing at different levels. All of which co-exist in harmony with each other, and constantly enrich the vibrant world which is the soil. In this way, the potential to fuel growth is maximised, creating a happy medium for the plants. This is the key to organic horticulture. The practice of digging (i.e. inverting of the soil) can disrupt this delicate balance, and the process of achieving equilibrium has to be started all over again. However, digging is acceptable in cases of compacted or poor quality soils, and the use of a fork is preferred to that of a spade.

Much is recycled on site, potash from fires, clippings and leaf mould all are composted and larger branches and wooden stems shredded for use on bark paths.

Consideration is also given to the attraction of wildlife: - the flutter of butterflies' wings; the buzzing of busy bees; the hurried scurrying of beetles and ants; and the dulcet tones of birdsong stir the heart, and soothe the mind. The planting leans away from formalism towards the more natural feel of a cottage garden. Preference is for native and

Previous pages:
The waterfall in Arthur's
Court and Purple Clover.
Above: The path to the
Well.

Top: The newly created
physik garden.
Below: Jerusalem Sage.

indigenous species rather than exotic, or tropical plants. Clashing colours, or too striking a contrast of shape, could feel too discordant. The garden is a pilgrimage destination and a space for contemplation and meditation and therefore the planting seeks to reflect harmony, balance and calm.

With Chalice Well being a place of Sanctity, Peace and Healing, there has been a renewed interest in recent years of the healing properties of plants and a subsequent establishing of a medicinal "Physik" herb garden. Herbs include Arnica, Echinacea, Calendula, Skullcap, Mugwort, Valerian, Hypericum, Agrimony, Evening Primrose, Lavender, Purple Sage, Wormwood, Sweet Cicely *(Myrrhis odorata)*, nettle-leaved Bell Flower, Rue, Corncockle, Red Campion, Lady's Mantle, Goat's Rue, Sweet Woodruff, Lungwort, Mullein, Borage, Orange Hawkweed and Chives.

Also included are plants traditionally used for dyeing, such as Woad, Madder, Weld and Dyer's Greenweed.

Amongst the herbs are also Poppies, Foxgloves, Catmint, Roses, Agastache, Hollyhocks, Marigolds, Love-in-a mist *(Nigella damascena)*, Cornflowers, Scabious and Viper's Bugloss *(Echium vulgare)*, as well as the large glaucous shrub, Jerusalem Sage *(Phlomis fruticosa)* with its masses of striking yellow flowers.

The presence of Pan and the elemental Devas and Fairies, particularly in the wilder parts of the garden and grounds, are tangible to those who are sensitive. Some that tend the gardens consciously seek to work in coop-eration with the devic realms in much the same way as Findhorn did in the 1980's.

Devas are considered to hold the blueprint for the perfect plant and with the creation of the right conditions and environment the plant is given every possible opportunity to reach its perfection. It is then the task of Nature Spirits who channel the creative force of the Universe to unfold the blueprint as the plant grows.

As the ceremonies and events that are held in the Garden follow the natural cycle of the seasons, so the Gardens serve as a visible reminder keeping all in touch with nature and her rhythms.

R. Ogilvie Crombie and the nature kingdom

R. Ogilvie Crombie was a contemporary of Wellesley Tudor Pole who worked with Peter and Eileen Caddy and Dorothy Maclean in the early days of the Findhorn Community in Scotland.

He was the person who made contact with Pan and the nature kingdom during the 1960's. In 1966 he was, aged 75, living in Edinburgh where he used to visit the Royal Botanic Gardens. In March that year, while sitting quietly, he saw a beautiful figure, about three feet tall, and said, "Hello." This figure told Crombie that he was a faun named Kurmos and he lived in the gardens to help the trees. He also said that the nature spirits had lost interest in the humans as the humans had stopped believing in nature spirits.

The following month, in a different location in Edinburgh, Crombie met with a huge presence who announced that he was Pan, one of the ancient gods. A few weeks later, on a visit to Iona, Crombie saw a large figure lying on the ground who again announced himself as Pan. "I am the servant of Almighty God and I and my subjects are willing to come to the aid of mankind in spite of the way he has treated us and abused nature, if he affirms belief in us and asks for our help."

Thus began a reconciliation between the Nature Kingdom and humanity. Crombie wrote that this relationship takes place outside of time and space.
He defined the following terms:

'**Devas**' design the archetypal pattern for each species and channel down the required energies for its manifestation on earth.
'**Nature spirits**' may be regarded as the builders – building the 'etheric counterpoint' from the energies channelled by the devas.
'**Elemental beings**' are actually whirls or vortices of energy that can appear to human eyes in the archetypal form of fauns, elves, spirits etc. Whatever is the easiest way for our brains to interpret the sensory information. Some people see them only as little bursts of light or colour.
'**Pan**' is a cosmic energy found throughout the whole of nature.

This information is taken from the following sources:
'**The Magic of Findhorn**' by Paul Hawken
'**The Findhorn Garden**' by The Findhorn Community
'**The Kingdom Within**' by Alex Walker
plus the ROC interview on BBC television with Magnus Magnusson in 1970

Above right: Original steps
leading from school
courtyard to the garden.
Above: The original
waterfall.

Part 2:   Chalice Well Garden Timeline

1958   "desolate and overgrown" after at least 14 years without
              a gardener

1959   laying of paths, planting of flowers, initial layout planned

1960–1966   archaeological digs around Well head area find ancient
              yew (300 AD), swimming pool built by Tor School,
              Arthur's Courtyard developed with waterfall, Lion's
              Head installed for drinking water. First borders estab-
              lished.

1966–1979   gardens only open March–October. Pair of Copper
              Beech and Silver Birch trees planted in memory of WTP,
              holy thorn 'flourishing', once the school demolished –
              extension of the garden through the present Courtyard
              doorway (1976), double gate and castellated bottom wall
              built, severe flooding (1979) washes away paths, plants
              and borders (damage estimated at £2,000). Vesica pool
              built (1976-77)

1980   lower lawn sown, old millstone from Devenish, Ireland installed.

1981   herb garden underway with paths

1982   new waterfall area to vesica pool maturing.

1983   new trellis work erected in various areas, restoration of Little St. Michael's back garden started after being overgrown for at least ten years.

1984   nursery begun for propagation, lawn mower purchased.

1986   first full time gardener employed – Pym de Grijff, new borders developed around the garden.

1987   vegetable garden 'reintroduced' behind Little St. Michael's with herbs and small plot for cut flowers (for the house), small greenhouse bought, Bach flower remedies and essential oils used to cure bacterial and fungal disease, botanical roses introduced, dogs (except guide dogs) banned.

1988   first coloured plans printed, Catherine Carter replaces Pym, new Garden Dept built on site of old open barn at bottom of garden (completed May 1989).

1989   paved area around the Lion's Head extended.

Top left: Original gated entrance.
Bottom: Legh gate and new paths.
Top: Creating new borders.

1990   Prince Charles surprise visit October, Ian Sargeant worked with Catherine Carter and when she left in early '91 took over.

1991   summer – Ian Sargeant leaves, Stephen George arrives November – large section of main footpath re-laid, new stonework around Well head.

Clockwise from top: New paths, Arthur's Courtyard in full blossom, Ark Redwood, Stephen George, Catherine Carter.

1992   most of boundary wall between Arthur's Court and Wellhouse Lane rebuilt, main well drainage pipe across lower lawn replaced, planting of 500 trees and shrubs as a shelterbelt across top of the meadow and Cress field, first signs of honey fungus.

The Gardens in the 1970's
and 1980's.

1993   Michael Eisele, arrives as landscaper and flowform installed.

1994   flooding over the winter, ground waterlogged.

1995   new herb garden behind Little St. Michael's.

1996   new stonework around well with more seating, whole area replanted to create 'a natural and secretive atmosphere around the Well', stone seat built in Arthur's Courtyard, rough stone path built to meadow, Michael Eisele carves new angel (replacing one stolen in 1991).

1997   new entrance built with pergola, gateway by shop becomes the new exit, 'plum orchard' planted with wide

variety of apple, pear, plum, meadow area planted with Daffodils, Bluebells and Grape Hyacinth, gardens opened to school parties.

1998   electric buggy purchased, various native trees planted in Meadow.

1999   Martin Faulkner replaces Michael Eisele.

2000   path built into Meadow and upper part of the field flattened, hazel arch erected between garden and Meadow, Stephen George leaves end of February, Ark Redwood joins.

2001   terracing the gardens at back of Vine Cottage and Little St. Michael's – creating sitting areas, chakra borders created with Pamela Woods.

2002   creation of new sanctuary reveals new springs – new pool created.

2004   first recognition of effect of climate change on garden, Gillan Cook arrives, more seating round wellhead, bird boxes, arbor seat from Chris Craig at top of garden, new rill built across lower lawn, new swing seat in meadow.

2005   Gillan replaced by Mike Stoltz as landscaper/handyman, new orchard in Tor field, 'the glade' created above Arthurs Court.

2006   willow on lower lawn dies, apples from Buckton's Orchard juiced for first time.

2007   handrails installed on walks and paths, herb garden developed into physik garden, sanctuary repaved by Martin.

2008   new shelter with wheelchair ramp, new front garden for Vine Cottage.

Above: Foxgloves in the Chakra Border.
Next page: The Holy Thorn.

Waterfall (with Orbs).

The Inner Garden

In 'The Awakening Letters' (1978) Cynthia Sandys and Rosamond Lehmann published 'The Glastonbury Scripts' which included channelled letters written by WTP at Chalice Well in February 1969 (about five months after his death). In one of the letters he describes the following,

"I saw a turbulence of beauty glow in the valley, and reach up, enveloping the Devas......the apricot light of Christ's aura grew and blended with the smoke-blue of the Glastonbury vibration. The two rays formed into a most astonishing pattern, resembling a huge flower with tendrils reaching out in all directions. I sat down and basked in the beauty and intensity of this experience."

For anyone attempting to understand Glastonbury and the Isle of Avalon it can be quite a journey. Pre-Christian Druids and Goddess culture lead to Joseph of Arimathea and the coming of Christ which lead on to the Grail and the Matter of Britain and into the spiritual revival of the twentieth century with Bligh Bond's psychical investigations, Maltwood's Zodiac, John Michell's 'City of Revelation' and the recent developments in contemporary spirituality including Broadhurst and Millers work on the Michael and Mary lines, Kathy Jones' Goddess work and Nicholas Mann's books on Glastonbury.

As we focus in on Chalice Well we can begin to see many layers of meaning held within its position between the Tor and Chalice Hill and its red and white waters that surface in its valley. Felicity Hardcastle wrote in the first garden booklet (1962):

"so Chalice Well combines in itself ideas from which all men can draw deep spiritual wisdom, healing and inspiration. Beneath the symbol is the Truth and to the future Percevals and Galahads and to all the pure in heart it shall indeed be revealed. Thus, not for the first time may ' Truth be found at the bottom of the Well."

So it is possible to walk the gardens in a meditative truth-seeking manner and in fact the gardens and the waters invite us to do so. Here we are walking the garden on another level, which is not entirely physical. This enables us to have access and contact with the eternal mystery. Each person will find their own path, their own way of walking and being. Offered here are some hints, some sharing, some gentle nudges and received wisdom.

Leaving busy Chilkwell Street with its heavy traffic we depart from the everyday world. Take time passing under the pergola 'to shake the dust off of your shoes' and remember all the pilgrims who came this way before you. After being welcomed at the gatehouse the pilgrim can turn right and stand on the lawn looking down at the vesica pool and flow form. Situated on the way to the shop and the exit from the gardens the symbolic pool holds the energy of the outer court in the gardens. Here we can watch the water swirling and moving, quietening awhile in the pool before making its way across the lawn on its journey to the Abbey. To the side of the pool on the lower slope is the Holy Thorn tree.

Just before the guardian Yews is the millstone from Devenish Isle. Take time to tune in to the links with Ireland and Iona and look back across the vale to the Holy Thorn on Wearyall Hill imagining the old arrivals on the quay at Weary-all. Now you enter the Inner Court of the garden between the magnificent old Yews. Acknowledge them as guardians; develop a relationship, tune-in to energies flowing up through the garden as the water flows down from the well.

Through the doorway in front of you, you glimpse the red waterfall in King Arthur's Courtyard. Step through the door after crossing the path, which leads to another Vesica shaped Yew, on the right, and soak up the atmosphere. To your right is the healing pool, which used to be deeper in days gone by. Despite the coldness of the water it is a wonderful experience to walk quietly through the pool, feeling the water flowing around you, holding on to the safety rail, or to just sit with your feet in the waters. Many healings have taken place here. Tudor Pole was particularly interested in this part of the garden and he writes in 'My Dear Alexias' how he has undertaken to create a type of etheric hospital around and above the Courtyard. He reports to Rosamond Lehmann that the mission was totally successful. There is a stone bench for contemplation and meditation and many people take time here

enjoying the sound of the waterfall and the visual interplay of light on the waters. Richard Leviton, Steiner scholar and editor of 'Alternative Medicine Digest' was inspired to write in one of his books, "Arthur's Courtyard was designed under guidance through inspiration in conscious light to sacred dimensions made with sacred measurements." He claims it will be used in the coming times as a meeting place between the worlds and focuses on the stairway (14 steps) which lead up to the Lion's Head, 'if you climb the stairway, consciously aware of stepping each step, there is an extraordinary experience available.' This is where the Michael and Mary energy lines cross paths as they make their way through Glastonbury from St. Michael's Mount in Cornwall to leave the east coast between Great Yarmouth and Lowestoft.

On climbing the steps you can drink from the Lion's Head under the aura of the second Holy Thorn. A few sips will suffice. Splash your chakras gently with the waters. Absorb the qualities of the water. The Lion is often found as a guardian at the gates and also links us back 12,000 years to the age of Leo. Then we take the fifty or so steps to the Legh gate, up the path towards the source. Beautiful flowers in the borders delight the senses and we can choose to rest and dream mid-way at the Angel seat. Butterflies and nature spirits often abound.

Within the energetic constructs of the garden lies the possibility of contacting the Wounded Fisher King and the Grail Castle. This is a complicated idea that would require a book on its own to do it justice. However, the writer Richard Leviton and others have explored this idea in relation to Glastonbury and Chalice Well pointing out that Glastonbury has potential as an energy matrix and that individuals and groups can work well within this matrix.

The Wounded Fisher King in the Wasteland is an expression of the spiritual hero who needs healing. The King's wound (often in the thigh area of the body) blocks the memory of his divine origin. While meditating at the Well one can imagine the rainbow bridge stretching from the Tor to the valley below (and Chalice Hill), which represents a bridge between this world and the next.

.Tudor Pole hinted that this was in fact a doorway to Shambhalla. According to WTP it was Joseph of Arimathea who 'saw' Albion''s destiny in Somerset *at the moment he burned the Cross in Palestine (on Mount Tabor?). WTP writes of this as a "stupendous vision" including "the future of the human race." And so Joseph was to plant the Piscean seed in Wearyall Hill for the future Aquarian flowering, in which Tudor Pole believed, Chalice Well would play its part at the opening of the new era. "Joseph's flowering staff illuminates the way to the New Jerusalem".*

Above the gate we see the brazier, some time holder of the amber light perpetual flame, which was re-lit at Winter Solstice 2007. Now we enter the Well head area. To the left is the Sanctuary with its clear water spring. A companion recently wrote, 'for me the sanctuary is a place that seems to glow and radiate with light – the love that radiates from the Divine Mother for her children who have come back to sit awhile with her.' To the right is the Well. Look into the waters and acknowledge the great Devic forces that dwell here at this ancient site. There are plenty of seats here for taking time and contemplation. Two more yew trees stand guard and signify the exit from the inner garden.

Returning to the outer court the path leads us up through the beech hedge and into the meadow. If you hadn't realised the gradual immersion in the deep energies of the garden as you walked around the paths it is now, upon entering the meadow, that you experience another considerable shift, as you walk on to the lower slopes of Chalice Hill rising out of the valley to look across to Wearyall Hill and the Tor. This meadow area was opened up so there was a place for talking with friends, having a picnic and letting children play on the grassy slopes. Here we can sit on the swing seat, watching the ancient Tor, and pondering our experience of walking the garden.

The Waters

In ancient times Logres was a rich country but it was turned into a Wasteland for the kingdom lost the voices of the wells and the damsels that were in them. These damsels would offer food and drink to wayfarers. A traveller had only to wish for food and seek out one of the wells and a damsel would appear from out of the well with the food he liked best, a cup of gold in her hand. No wayfarers were excluded from this service.
From *The Elucidation: a Prologue to the Conte del Graal.*

Water is the life blood of the Chalice Well. The Well head, the Lion's Mouth, Arthur's Courtyard, and the Vesica Piscis pool all provide sanctuaries for being with, listening to, contemplating or drinking water. In ancient times, when natural sources were the only supply of water, the springs and pools were revered and a spirit was said to dwell within them.

The writer of the *Lebor Gabala*, the Irish 'Book of Invasions,' said the original people "had a well around which grew the nine hazel trees of inspiration, poetry and wisdom. There were seven streams of wisdom flowing from that well and the people of art have all drunk from them." As well as these gifts, the wells also conferred great abundance on the Celtic peoples.

No Celtic chieftain could rule without the gift of sovereignty granted by the spirit of the land. For this reason, the wells and springs where this spirit dwelt were offered rich gifts, especially cups, shields and swords. King Arthur was no exception to this rule. He too sought the confirmation of his right to be king from stones and springs – that is, from the spirit that dwelt within the elements of the land itself.

What is Water?

We can see the power attributed to water in traditions like those quoted above, but what is water? Why should it have been given such special powers?

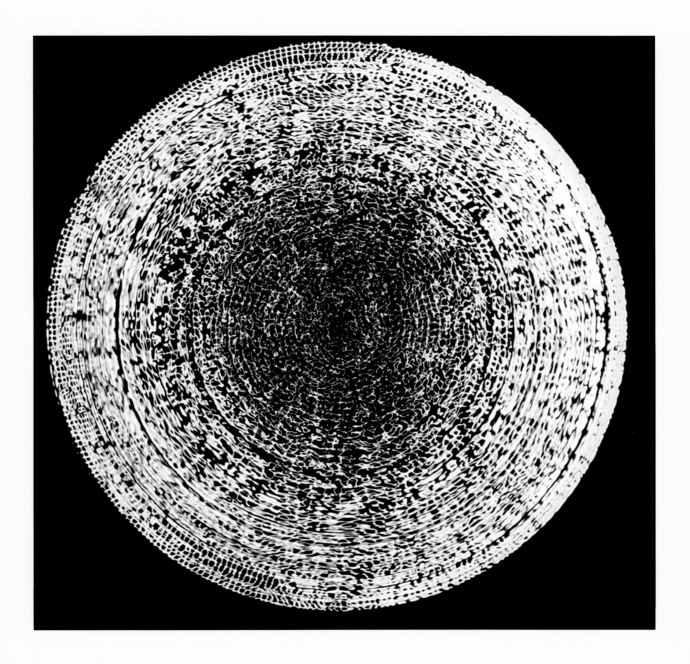

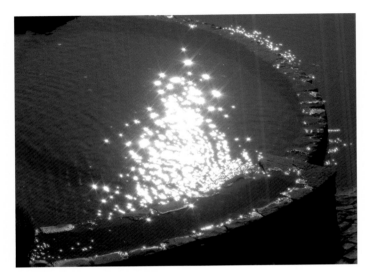

"Hydrogen can be viewed as a tiny light ethereal body which is very sociable but has a tendency to pull upwards, to aim for the skies," writes Charlie Ryrie author of *The Healing Energies of Water.* "Oxygen is equally sociable but tends to head downwards towards the Earth. At their meeting point they form the universal mediating element, water, with two light hydrogen atoms bonding to the heavier oxygen. Water is, if you like, the meeting point between heaven and Earth – it forms a cosmic connection…If hydrogen bonds were just a bit stronger, water would be solid at 100°C (212°F), then all life on Earth would cease to exist."

The above is a scientific description, but to *really* know what water is, you must feel it on your skin, experience it in your throat, contemplate its still, mirror-like surface or sit in silence, listening to it trickle over stones or thunder over the edge of a waterfall.

"The mystery of language was revealed to me," wrote Helen Keller, blind and deaf from the age of nineteen months, "When I knew that 'w-a-t-e-r' meant the wonderful cool something that was flowing over my hand. That living word awakened my soul, gave it light, joy, set it free!"

The History of Water and its Healing Power

In many myths of the world 'water' appears as the central theme of the genesis of creation; nevertheless it is not to be equated with today's element 'water.' The liquid primordial ocean is not something 'arisen,' but the expression of pure becoming and 'forming,' a flowing, streaming medium, of the archetypal, embryonic world-seed as living, pulsating vibration.
Alexander Lauterwasser, Water Sound Images

No matter which ancient culture, or religious tradition, we explore, we find myths about the sanctity of water, and practices to connect with its

Water-Sound-Image, sound inside a well by Alexander Lauterwasser.
Above: Light reflecting on the Vesica Pool.

power. The Sumerian word *mar* meant sea and *womb*, and the Hebraic ideogram *Mem* designated mother, life, womb and sea. To this day baptism in water is, for Christians, a universal symbol of purification and regeneration.

> "For the itch, the stitch, rheumatic, and the gout,
> If the devil isn't in you, this well will take it out".
> Ancient healing rhyme
> Quoted by Janet and Colin Bord in '*Sacred Waters*'

But the Second Council of Arles decreed: "If in the territory of a bishop, infidels light torches or venerate trees, fountains or stones, and he neglects to abolish this usage, he must know that he is guilty of sacrilege." Despite the efforts of the early Roman church to stop people praying at springs and wells, the practice flourishes to this day; with renewed strength, if anything, as the extraordinary healing powers of water are more widely recognised and appreciated.

In *Sacred Waters* Janet and Colin Bord listed seventy-five different illnesses which attributed their cure to water from holy wells, with eye problems being the most common. This may be because bathing the eyes with holy water cured 'smoke eyes' from living in smoky cottages. But Wellesley Tudor Pole went further than this, writing in 1948 that water from a healing spring should be used for "bathing the eyes of those who desire their inner and outer vision to be renewed."

There is a subtler, more profound dimension to water-as-healer which lies in its capacity to store and transmit *energetic information*. "Water from a particular Well or Source never loses its affinity for the place from which it has been taken," wrote Wellesley Tudor Pole:

> "If, for instance, a trained psychometrist handles water taken from a special spring he will find himself in contact with that spring and its surroundings, even if the sample of water he is handling has been carried a thousand miles away. This curious property of water is well known in the East… a Caravan passing through the Arabian Desert may come across a water hole that shows signs of drying up or becoming brackish and

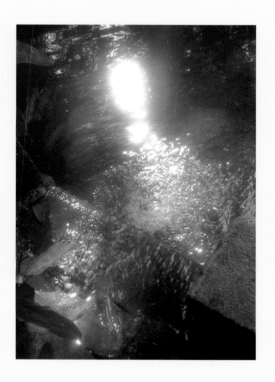

Angel in the water.
Opposite: Easter Healing
Ceremony in Arthur's
Courtyard.

undrinkable. The leader of the Caravan will carry a sample of this water with him until he meets a Holy Man or saintly hermit. The latter will be asked to bless this water, perhaps at a place situated hundreds of miles away from the water hole from which it was taken. As a result it transpires that the original water hole will often renew itself in a way that cannot be explained by human reasoning."

WTP, **"The Healing Properties of Water"** 1948.

Where does Chalice Well water come from?

Wella is the Anglo Saxon word for 'spring.' The Chalice Well is actually a spring, and said to be the oldest continuously used Holy Well in Britain. 25,000 gallons of water flow through the gardens every day in winter (around 19,000 in summer) – enough to fill about 555 average-sized bathtubs! It has never been known to fail, even in the severe droughts of 1921-22 when household water supplies were turned off from 5 p.m. and the swimming pool in nearby Wells was forced to close. But where does all this water come from?

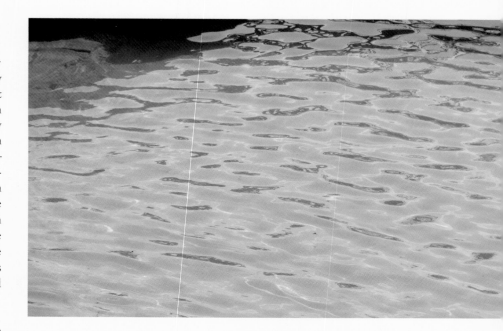

Nicholas Mann is convinced that the water originates in a two-layer aquifer replenished by rainfall within the adjacent Tor, the bottom layer of which contains iron - the source of the chalybeate water which flows into the Chalice Well. "The water," he says, "does not have a distant origin but, in fact, gains its power by being home-brewed!" On the other hand, Sig Lonegren has dowsed sacred sites around the globe and he thinks the Chalice Well water is *primary* water. "Primary water doesn't come from above. It comes from below,"

he explains. "So it is not dependent on rainfall and it begins its existence way down in the bowels of our Mother, the Earth, and is usually the result of chemical processes."

Holy Water – Healing Water

The writer of 'The Elucidation', the Grail romance quoted at the beginning of this chapter, described how the ruler was bound to protect the maidens of the wells. But he told how King Amangons broke this custom: "Although it was his duty to guard the damsels and keep them within his peace, he raped one of them and took away her golden cup for his own service. After that time no damsel was seen issuing from a well... and the service of the wells ceased."

This tradition, that the ancient wells originally poured forth not just water, but abundance, inspiration, poetry and even sovereignty, was preserved upon the Isle of Avalon for much longer, it seems, than elsewhere. The Chalice Well in its protected location seems to have been venerated as a source of these things long after they had ceased to be found at other wells. Not only was Joseph of Arimathea said to have come to Avalon with his cup, but legend also reports that near here King Arthur was given the sword that conferred him with sovereignty, by the 'Lady of the Lake'. Eventually, the sword was returned to the waters of Avalon for concealment and repair. But this was only after Arthur's knights had set out on their greatest quest of all: to find the golden cup, the Holy Grail that healed the Wasteland.

Why did the spring in the centre of Avalon become identified with the Grail quest, as a surviving symbol of the bond between the wells of the land and the rightful king? In Arthurian legend, Avalon is the place where the wounded king went for healing and there waits, not dead, but sleeping. Whatever one feels about this myth, Glastonbury, for many remains a holy place, a place of great healing power.

Wellesley Tudor Pole wrote, "When water wells up from hidden springs and sources and is brought intimately into contact with air, such water always possesses healing and vitalising qualities which vary in strength mainly according to the rhythm of the mineral substances through which the water has passed in its pilgrimage from darkness into the light of day."

From reports in the Chalice Well Gatehouse Day Book and from letters received, many Companions and visitors share stories of the healing effects of drinking or bathing in the water. Several have reported the improvement of troublesome skin conditions – from walkers delighted that blisters disappeared after bathing their feet in the Healing Pool, to more complex conditions - such as a metal allergy being healed. Willa Sleath, a former Guardian, was amazed to witness a woman being cured of psoriasis after bathing her hands at the Lion's Head and under the waterfall in Arthur's Court. A man was hospitalized with acute industrial dermatitis, but was able to discharge himself after bathing with water from Arthur's Court. Gangesh Kumari Kak found the water healed both herself and her animals – and now, when she returns to India, she pours it into *her* well.

Ned Reiter, former President of the National Institute of Medical Herbalists, cautions against drinking chalybeate water *in quantity* because excess iron gets deposited in the liver, heart, pancreas and pituitary gland, with potentially damaging results.

Above: Sound Water Healing at Chalice Well's Healing Weekend.
Opposite: Pouring waters of the World into the Well to celebrate World Water Day.

In 2006 eleven children from Chernobyl spent an afternoon at Chalice Well. They passed a chalice of Well water around and directed their thoughts and wishes into it. The water was then poured into the Well with the intention of carrying their prayers out into the world. Each child was given a bottle of Chalice Well water to pour into springs, rivers and water courses around Chernobyl when they returned home.

Making remedies from the water

"I call the water holy," says Sig Lonegren, "because it comes straight from the Mother. It's pure in the sense that it's full of the spirit and hasn't been messed up by man's chemical 'purification' process." Sig has a homeopathic collection of water, from holy wells all over the world. "You don't need a lot to make it work," he says "– a drop in a glass of water is sufficient."

Sophie Knock makes flower essences, mixing water from the red and white springs at the Full Moon. This creates a 'rosé' from the French word for dew, *rosée,* which symbolises the heart and the alchemy of unity-consciousness. *The Holy Thorn* remedy, sold in the shop at Chalice Well, is also made from the Well water.

Helios Homeopathic Pharmacy has created a Chalice Well remedy, and Ian White, of Australian Bush Flower Essences, makes his Devic Essence with Chalice Well water. Steve Johnson, founder of Alaskan Flower Essences created an environmental essence in the early 1980's. Madeleine Evans (who created a homeopathic remedy from Chalice Well water) says it encourages stillness and surrender. Wellesley Tudor Pole recommended taking 'seven drops in a tumbler of ordinary drinking water or milk,' at times of illness.

The Commercial Question

In the early years of the Trust, there was a passionate debate about whether or not to sell Chalice Well water. In the 1970s, discussions took place about bottling it for export, and the Trust was contacted by

Grayshott Hall who wanted to supply 90 patients every week with Chalice Well water. The matter was finally laid to rest in a letter from John Simmons to Ivan Landau, Solicitor, on 7 April 1976: "The Chalice Well Trustees, at their meeting on 6th April, instructed me to say unequivocally that they do not wish to enter into an agreement with anyone for the sale of water from the Chalice Well Spring. This being so there is no basis for further discussion…" However, WTP never categorically ruled out the selling of the waters if the need arose.

Water on Earth and Water in our Bodies

Healthy water has a strong three-dimensional crystalline microstructure that allows it to collect and transmit information. It is the structure of the water that allows it to communicate.
Charlie Ryrie, The Healing Energies of Water

Caroline 'A-Mira' Wyndham has, for over 25 years, worked in co-operation with the mineral kingdom; travelling to many places in the world to assist in grounding the new blueprint into the crystalline grid system of the Earth. She explains the significant link (for healing and evolution) between planetary water and water in the human body: "As a cranio sacral worker, I work a lot with water in the body. The cerebro-spinal fluid is so necessary in its function for our health and wellness, because it carries the light codes of information. What now seems to be happening is the activation of the pineal and pituitary glands. The pineal gland is the gland which receives the light codes of information that we need for the changes - and the same is happening within the planet. So, as we activate our own new consciousness — our new awareness of ourselves as connected to a greater source of creation — then we can bring that, through our prayer, *intention* and work, into the planet.

These new codes, (new light informational and vibrational frequencies) come into the planet through the oceans which flow and connect all continents. In our bodies, the cerebro-spinal fluid connects all our organs, tissues, muscles and every activity of bodily function, which is why we are experiencing rather strange, and sometimes unrecognisable, symptoms! New parts of our cellular memory are being activated and

Above: Pendant created to hold the Chalice Well Water in order that it can be carried about the person emitting its healing energies.

seeded." These words from a contemporary planetary light-worker echo those of the great 'Water Wizards' of the past – Rudolf Steiner, Theodor Schwenk and Viktor Schauberger. "When our pineal gland is sparked, and it resonates," Caroline continues, "then it can actually bring that frequency, that vibration, into the body and *ignite* the cells, because there is an etheric blueprint within us. That is where water has a very important place, because it can carry the total memory of the original blueprint from billions of years ago when this planet came into being."

World Water Day

At the Spring Equinox 2005 the United Nations instigated the *Decade of Water* and, since then, an annual ceremony has taken place at Chalice Well to celebrate World Water Day. On 25 July 2006 Caroline 'A-Mira' Wyndham, a regular visitor to the Well for over twenty years, conducted a healing water ceremony in Tel-Aviv. Caroline opened the ceremony by adding water she had brought from Chalice Well to water from the Sea of Galilee. Meanwhile, back in England, at the Well head in Glastonbury, Sophie Knock was conducting a simultaneous ceremony.

"Today," Sophie said, "we've come together to join many other people around the world to offer our love and thanks to the water that flows inside and outside our bodies. Let us visualize the vibration of love and thanks as golden/silver light. Let us see that light filling our hearts and overflowing into the waters of Chalice Well. From there let us see that light joining the rivers and streams and going into the sea, from where it rises again as rain and falls all over the earth – suffusing the whole earth with this golden/silver light."

Both ceremonies concluded with the participants saying:

Water we love you.

Water we thank you.

Water we respect you.

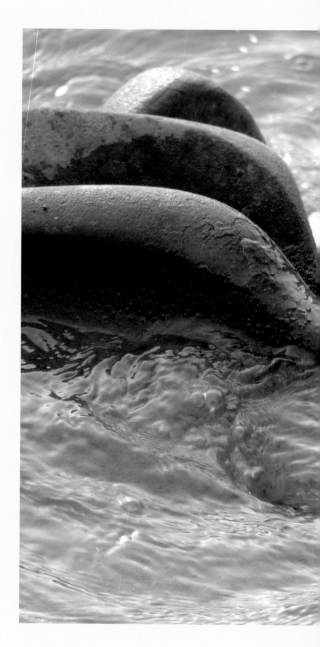

There are many ceremonies that honour the water at the Chalice Well today. Sooner or later, the pilgrim to Chalice Well will encounter the Grail question, "Whom does the Grail serve?" As we connect with the spirit of the land at sacred places, especially at the wells that distil its essential nature, we discover that this gift can never be bought, appropriated or taken by force. Rather, like the water of the original springs of the land, it is freely offered to all. By acknowledging this deep spiritual truth, and by giving our thanks, love and reverence back to the waters, we not only help to heal the Wasteland. We also heal ourselves.

Flowform

In its natural, self-cooling, spiralling, convo-luting motion, water is able to maintain its vital inner energies, health and purity. In this way it acts as the conveyor of all the necessary minerals, trace elements and other subtle energies to the surrounding environment. Naturally flowing water seeks to flow in darkness or in the diffused light of the forest, thus avoiding the damaging direct light of the sun.' It forms 'in-winding, longitudinal, clockwise–anti-clockwise alternating spiral vortices down the central axis of the current, which constantly cool and re-cool the water, maintaining it at a healthy temperature and leading to a faster, more laminar, spiral flow.

Viktor Schauberger

I would like to say loud and clear that it is a vitally important social task today to work on the idea that water is our most precious resource for which humankind needs to develop a universal and alert consciousness…the water cycle has maintained itself as a life-giving resource for millennia by means of its ability to move water through many different states. These states have to do with constant movement, and even more specifically with rhythmic movement, together with a quality of surface that is intimately connected with life processes. In a word, all organisms are connected and associated through water…The next generation must develop a completely new attitude to water if survival in many arid parts of the world is to be guaranteed, and indeed the same necessity applies to maintenance of the quality of life in industrialized nations.

John Wilkes

In July 1967 the Warden, John Simmons, wrote to Wellesley Tudor Pole, '…in any treatment of the Chalice Spring Water we should pay attention to the findings of Theodor Schwenk who is the Director of an Institute located at Herrischried in the Black Forest…I feel now that we should consult him because my original approach to this problem as a simple construction job has now been turned topsy-turvy…we really need the advice of someone who knows about the properties of water and we should really know what we are doing if we aerate it.'

John Wilkes, who designed the flowform above the Vesica Piscis, first heard of the work of Rudolf Steiner in 1951 and later studied with Schwenk at the Institute for Flow Sciences. He writes, 'It has been to Schwenk's work…to which I owe the inception of my own design and scientific research. His seminal contribution to the reawakening of a true modern consciousness for water is fundamental to the contents of the present book, which I consider in all humility as the description of one consequence of his investigative research.'

He calls his book, '"Flowforms, 'the biography of an idea'" which started for him when he was sitting on the shore of a Scottish loch: 'All at once

I became aware of the great in-breathing motion of the whole ocean surface rising. This was a rare and unusual experience of the tide rising visibly, inexorably to the slow rhythm of the beckoning Moon…The land was drawing up its mantle of water.' In noticing the wave pattern caused by a protruding rock, a stream entering a pool in a straight line then flowing into a 'meandering rhythmical swing,' he observed three very different patterns of rhythm in water – known as laminar, harmonic and turbulent.

The key thing that Wilkes achieved was to discover how to generate rhythms in streaming water by means of a specified level of resistance. 'Water and surface are inseparable,' he writes. 'Water is always moving over surfaces, and, over shorter or longer periods, depending on the erodible nature of the material, the shape of those surfaces is influenced. Water in movement also tends to create a multitude of surfaces within itself but these can be influenced by the condition of the water. In a living context water movement plays a major creative role in formative processes. Indeed, every physical forming process is at some time in a fluid state.'

Flowforms can be stone or ceramic and are inserted into a water course to oxygenate and energize the water. They reflect the natural flow pattern that water creates in a stream or river, and also that of blood flowing round the heart. Water, coursing in a rhythmic double figure of eight through a flowform, creates double vortexes occur along its path, and it is these which energize the water.

This is an extract from the original Chalice Well guidebook written by Felicity Hardcastle in the early 1960's:

Construction of the Well

Chalice Well is fed by a spring which rises on the slope of Chalice Hill and gives an outflow of 25,000 gallons a day. The water is chalybeate (impregnated with iron) and beautifully clear. The well itself is built of massive stones and forms two chambers, the inner one being reached through an opening at the foot of the western wall of the shaft. The whole structure is orientated roughly north and south.

The Well-shaft, approximately 3ft x 3ft 5in, is constructed from large squared blocks of local lias, some retaining traces of diagonal tooling. The total depth is 9ft; the lower 5ft of the walls are apparently undisturbed, but above this the blocks project irregularly with cut –away and worn surfaces. It is suggested that these upper stones are the remains of a corbelled roof. Above these stones there has been some heightening in more recent times, up to the level of the present concrete surround. The walls of the shaft are bonded at the corners; the joints are tight and there are some remains of what appears to be the original mortar between the stones.

Dr. Ralegh Radford considers that the character of the stones on the well-shaft is consistent with a date in the 12th century before A.D. 1184, or with a re-use of stones salvaged from the Abbey shortly after the disastrous fire that year. It has been found that a water supply coming from the direction of Chalice Well was introduced into the new extensions to the Monastery built about A.D. 1220.

The date of the inner chamber, or even its real purpose, is still uncertain. It is suggested that it may have been constructed about A.D. 1750 with later additions cir. 1820. Its possible use was as a sedimentation tank to ensure a clean supply to the pilgrims' bathing pool in the garden below and the Pump-room in the town. It is also interesting to note that this very peculiar pentagonal shaped chamber could have been built on very ancient foundations, as the old measurements employed relate to those used by the Egyptians and the architects of both prehistoric and very early Christian buildings.

A suggestion has been made that these well chambers were originally above ground, but in the course of time, rain and earthquakes in the 13th century have brought down the soil from the hillside above and they have become silted over and completely covered. Colour is given to this theory by results of the excavations on the site directed by Mr. P.A. Rahtz in 1961. In a section cut away during these excavations, the stones on the outside of the chamber were found to have been chiselled to a fine finish.

At the bottom of a trench just east of the Well, nearly 12ft below the present surface, the stump of a yew tree was found. This had a fine tap-root and part of the trunk, in all some 2ft 6in long. It was found in a layer of blue-grey clay, and clearly was in situ where it had formerly grown. A specimen was sent to Leeds University where it was tested for water content and found to have been a living tree in Roman times, cir. A.D. 300. This suggests that the ground level at that period was approximately the same as the present bottom of the Well and that the water came out as a surface spring. Whether or not this spring was covered by any structure or wood or stone, either at that date or in the subsequent centuries, cannot be proved without very extensive excavations which the Trustees at present think undesirable. At least we now have indications that this site was frequented from earliest times. Mr. Rahtz found several dozen flints (upper Palaeolithic or Mesolithic) and a shard of Iron Age pottery – the first to be found in Glastonbury outside the famous Lake Villages. Roman and medieval shards were also found in more recent layers.

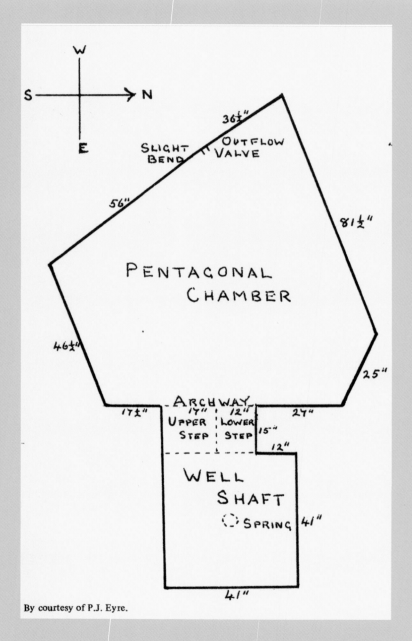

By courtesy of P.J. Eyre.

INTERIOR OF CHALICE WELL.   20563

It is most interesting to note that the yew tree stump was in a line with the other yews now growing at the well, and on the two lower terraces of the slope. Is this coincidence, or does it indicate the track of some very ancient ritual path up this valley?

The Natural Spring has been capped to ensure its purity. From the Well-head the water is piped down under the terraced garden and comes out for the first time at the Lion's Head, the only place in the gardens where it is now safe to drink. We see the water again gushing forth not far from the Lion's Head as a delightful little terraced waterfall which in past centuries filled a pool where sufferers came to bathe in the healing waters. The water then goes through an underground piping system.

The water can then be traced along Chilkwell Street to the top of Bere Lane and thence into the Abbey grounds. It may have filled the Pilgrim Well in St. Joseph's Chapel before crossing under Magdalene Street to supply the Pump Room and Bath House built in 1752. Some of the hollow tree trunks once used as pipes can still be seen in the Abbey Museum.

The Spring has never been known to fail and in the dry years of 1921-22 it was the sole means of saving the whole town from drought. Water is available anytime from a spout coming from the garden wall on Well House Lane.

Interior shot of Chalice Well.
Opposite: Diagram of
pentagonal chamber.

'The Michael Sword and Dragon' commissioned by WTP, now lives in Little St. Michael's Retreat House.

Aerial view.

The Buildings and Their History

Parapsychologist *Rupert Sheldrake* writes on Morphic Resonance; "The influence of previous structures of activity on subsequent similar structures of activity organized by morphic fields. Through morphic resonance, formative causal influences pass through or across both space and time, and these influences are assumed not to fall off with distance in space or time, but they come only from the past. The greater the degree of similarity, the greater the influence of morphic resonance. In general, morphic units closely resemble themselves in the past and are subject to self-resonance from their own past states."

Many believe that buildings embody a spirit of place and this in turn can be affected by or even subtly influence the lives of those who live in them. On researching the buildings residing on the site, it is interesting to discover how, over the course of time, they weave themselves into the fabric of the story of Chalice Well. May Cottages, the Anchor Inn, Tor House are named among a number of buildings and dwellings in records and annals and their stories perhaps can be seen as a reflection of the subtle energies of the Well itself.

Some of those that lived here appear to have in some way worked with the waters, whether running laundries or healing spas or even working on the nearby White Spring Reservoir. Hospitality of one kind or another has always been offered here. The Anchor Inn, no doubt, welcomed pilgrims into the town who had passed through the nearby Toll House. Alice Buckton ran the Chalice Well Hostel and in more recent years the Chalice Well Trust has provided a place of Retreat. The buildings have also been home to educational establishments and activities, both spiritual and temporal and at one time was home to a chapel for prayer and worship.

Early Dwellings

The earliest recorded dwelling is referred to in an original guide book "The Chalice Well; A Short History" by F. Hardcastle 1962.

"The place name Chalcwelle is mentioned in connection with the family of Pasturel who were the Hereditary Bakers to the Abbey and had held that office since the time of Abbot Turstin (AD. 1079 – 1101)."

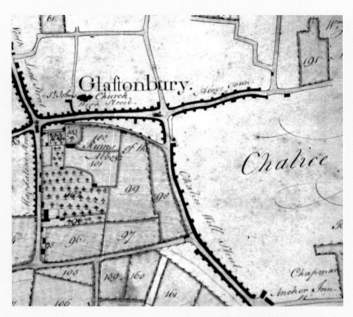

In the year 1117, Hugh Pasturel was granted land on which to build a house to be his family's perpetual possession in the town. The site was described as "where the Salt-works were." In later documents, the Pasturel property is described as "lying by iself next the highway (viam regiam) on the east side, which runs from Chalkwelle towards Edgaresley." John, son of Matthew the Master Baker (1189) married Muriel de Lavandria, whose family were the Hereditary Launderers and whose property seems also to have been close around the Well. This would certainly be a very natural site for such a purpose and the mention of an adjacent "Wullhouse" suggests that perhaps they also washed the fleeces there. Little more is known about the buildings on the site until several hundred years later.

May Cottages

As the housing developed in the neighbourhood of Chalice Well, the house numbering changed. The three terraced cottages are dated in part to the sixteenth century and both the 1891 and 1901 census refer to them as May Cottages. These are currently named as May Cottage, Vine Cottage and Little St. Michaels. Their respective house numbers today 85 – 89 Chilkwell Street, have over the course of time altered to accommodate the growing neighbourhood. 1844 County Tithing Records

Top: Close up crop of 1770's Survey Map showing Chalice Well Street.
Above: May Cottages circa 1920's.

Top: Renovations to Little St.
Michael's.
Top right: May Cottages.

provide information as to their ownership and appearance;

"1844 Tythe No 1642 house & garden owned by Dowell Rawles and occupied by William Applin
1844 Tythe No 1643 house & garden owned by Dowell Rawles
Situated in a cul-de-sac leading off Chilkwell Street.
Probably late C17 plus attics to right. Coursed rubble and ashlar. Pantile roofs. 3 dormers to No 89. 6 windows. Wood casements of 2 lights each, glazing bars. No 87 has one bay window of 3 lights to ground floor. Plain wooden door to right, No 89 has a wooden stable door."

The 1901 census offers a window onto the lives of the people who inhabited each of the 4 roomed "two up, two down" cottages;

John, a hired factory hand worker, his wife Emily Harper and their 2 year old daughter, Kathleen, lived in number 69 with relative Charles Harper also a Factory worker and "Rug Dresser".

Number 70 was home to Fred and Emily Green and their 6 children, Alice, Frank, George, Isabella, Rose and Fred junior aged from 14 to 2 years old. Fred was a Labourer on the Waterworks and may have been connected to the Reservoir (now known as the White Spring) across Wellhouse Lane run or the Upper Brue Drainage Board Offices in Chilkwell Street.

William Higgins and his Wife Emily lived at number 71 with 87 year old Joyce Coles. William was an Engine Stoker.

There is little more information other than a note in the archives which indicates that May Cottage was rented to a Mr. McMillan in the 1960's. Little St. Michael's was acquired by the Chalice Well Trust in 1961 from the Tor School, and it was Christine Sandeman who, in stalwart fashion esconced herself amidst the various works and repairs. Cynthia Legh writes of her in the Trust's Journal, *Messenger no. 24*:

"Sir, I feel I must express my real appreciation and admiration for Mrs. Sandeman's enthusiasm and friendliness in the days of founding the Chalice Well Trust. I suppose most people now linked with us, never knew her, but much gratitude to her is sincerely due.

We all went through very hard times together and when Little St. Michael's was but a damp, cold shell of a house, half of the walls cumbered with workment and ladders – she camped in it!

She was always ready to laugh through the hardships and set-backs, and to hold the great vision of the future. She gave a welcome to all who came, mostly with a cup of tea too!"

The Anchor Inn

This building, now no longer standing, was known by several names in its lifetime, Tor House, Torr Hill House, Tor Hill Inn and "The Anchor Inn".

In the 1962 guide to Chalice Well, Hardcastle writes about the origin of the name for the Anchor Inn which she relates to the story of Joseph of Arimathea coming to Glastonbury with 12 disciples.

"We are told that when the first Twelve died, others took their place, so the circle of huts continued until the days of St. Patrick who, about A.D. 400, persuaded these Anchorites to join together in one community and live henceforth the Monastic life in a building adjacent to the original Wattle Church."

But the memory of the twelve cells remained and the name of "The Anchorage" for an early building in the vicinity of the Well perpetuated the tradition. In later years, this became known as "The Anchor Inn," and as recently as 1910, there was a "Tor Hill Inn" at the foot of Well House Lane, to carry on this memory."

A map drafted by surveyor, John Davidge in 1799, of the land belonging to George Cox in Glastonbury and Meare, indicates two buildings at Chalice Well, one of which is named "Anchor Inn", the other we can identify as May Cottages. Both are situated on "Chalice Well Street",

Right: Rear of Tor House – Summer School 1915.

which is clearly marked, suggesting the current name Chilkwell may have derived from the name "Chalice Well".

At the foot of Well House Lane, The Anchor Inn (renamed Tor House) is clearly visible on the map, the Seminary or school building is yet to be erected.

Lodged in the National Archives are Deeds of the early 1800's which refer to "Tor House formerly the Anchor Inn in Chilkwell" as "a messuage and tenement " attached to "certain parcels of land, the Glastonbury mineral spring, etc".

An 1844 tithe survey shows the Anchor Inn belonging to a Mr James Croker, who also appears to have owned the Well and former Spa building; "1844 Tythe No 1646 garden & baths".

The description given is of a: "Large Gothic house of about 1830, with storey extensions to each side. Rendered, with ashlar dressings. Moulded cornices and crenellated parapets. Banded quoins to left-hand and some to right. Pantile and slate roofs. 4 windows with rectangular hoodmoulds. Sashes with glazing bars. One 3-light window with stone mullions to left on 1st floor. 3 bays of 3 lights each to ground floor. 2 ashlar bays with cornices and crenellated parapets to left (one bay with French windows). One modern wooden door to right."

Letters to Lord Glastonbury and General Grenville mention the Anchor Inn with bath and spring being bought by a Mr Bull for a glove factory. It was about 50 years later that a further building was erected on the Corner of Wellhouse Lane and Chilkwell Street to house the Missionaries of the Order of the Sacred Heart.

The School

With a rather austere and imposing exterior, the school building shown on records as "Tor House" stood on the corner of Chilkwell Street and Wellhouse Lane. As far as is known, there was always some form of educational establishment resident in the building.

The earliest records that we have indicate that it was built in the late 19th Century by a The Missionaries of the Sacred Heart who were a Roman Catholic congregation of priests and lay brothers. Their principle object was to promote the knowledge and practice of devotion to the Heart of Jesus primarily through missionary and educational work. The society's motto is "May the most Sacred Heart of Jesus be loved everywhere" and it was founded at Issoudun in the Archdiocese of Bourges, France, by the Abbe Jules Chavalier in 1864. The governing office was based in Rome with centres in other countries such as the United States, Canada, Australia, Ireland, Italy, Germany, Holland, Belgium and Switzerland. The order was introduced to Somerset by Bishop Clifford of Clifton in the 1880s.

The building became the Community House and its chapel was a place of worship for Roman Catholics in the Glastonbury community. Public services were held in the chapel on Sunday and holidays of obligation. Holy Communion was at 8am, Mass at 10.30am and benediction at 6.30pm. There was also a daily Mass took place at 7am.

The building also housed the 'Apostolic School' which was a 'junior seminary' providing basic education for its pupils who, it was hoped, would subsequently enter vocational training for the priesthood.
In the 1891 census we find their names listed and these boys and young

Top: Seminary.
Above: The original
bath house in King
Arthur's Court.

.

men ranged in age from 11 to 21. They had come from across the country and the tutors were gathered from the other centres of the Missionary in Europe. Head of the Glastonbury mission was Fr. John Power D.D. Superior, a 31 year priest of Irish descent.

In 1900 the school was closed and the missionary's Novitiate moved from France to Glastonbury. The fathers finally left in December 1910 and in March 1912, Tor House was put up for sale.

During their time at Tor House, the Fathers were very hospitable and allowed the public to visit the well. For 'an offering' to the Apostolic School, they would send bottled Chalice Well water to the donor.

In 1913 Alice Buckton bought the school buildings from the Order and continued a tradition of offering hospitality at Chalice Well. Here is an excerpt from a four page leaflet dated 1913 advertising Chalice Well as a Training College for women.

"Chalice Well Glastonbury (lately known as Tor House). A College for the Training of Gentelwomen for Dedicated Work. (Undenominational) The Chalice Well Hostel is in a wing of the building which has been simply fitted up for pilgrims and travellers, offering board and lodging at 25 – 35 shillings per week for women, and 27 – 37 shillings per week for men. (No extras). Supper, bed and breakfast with use of the bathroom, refectory, parlour and garden from 4 shillings per day. The chapel is open daily for silent prayer and meditation. The well spring will be uncovered each day at noon".

Following Alice Buckton's tenure, the building once more became a boys school and during the second world war homed evacuees including Field Marshall Lord Vincent, who, having re-visited Chalice Well in 2002, wrote the following recollections;

"So what, on reflection all these years later, are my lasting memories of the school and the historic town in which it was located? ... We did not make any school visits to the Abbey in my time, but the legends and history of Glastonbury inevitably grew in our consciousness over a period of five years. Indeed, with the Chalice Well in our grounds, and its water providing all domestic supplies for the school, that is hardly surprising. And every time we climbed the Tor we saw Wearyall Hill and became aware of the stories of Joseph of Arimathea, including the planting of his staff on stepping out of his boat, which gave birth to Glastonbury's Holy Thorn of which we had a large thriving offshoot in the school grounds… The photograph to which I referred earlier, which was taken of me and other boys around the Chalice Well over sixty years ago, seems at first sight to reveal a rather unkempt garden at that time but that is not my overall recollection. I remember the well chamber being carefully opened so that it could be examined and cleaned – a task to which I contributed by being sent down the well shaft and into the pentagonal chamber for which I still have clear memories today. I can still see the glistening orange coatings on that ancient masonry left by deposits of iron that had accumulated from the millions of gallons of that unique spring water that had flowed through the Chalice Well over the centuries. No doubt some of the other rich 'deposits' of Glastonbury's long and colourful history also settled on me during my unexpected but memorable sojourn at Glaston Tor School in the 1940s for which I shall always be most grateful."

Retreat Houses

"Drinking in the Solitude and reviving energies of the Chalice Well Gardens", *(Companion's newsletter The Chalice Well No.4., 1984)*

Understandably, there have been many who wished to stay a while in the beauty and tranquillity of the Well and gardens and the provision of a welcoming and peaceful space at Chalice Well for rest and retreat became one of the key activities of the Chalice Well Trust.

In the Messenger journal no.29 issued in the 1970's the following was offered by the then Warden John Simmons.
"Short-stay bed and breakfast accommodation will be available at Little St. Michael's, Chalice Well from Easter to Michaelmas: Single room £2.50: double room (single-bedded) £4.00: a simple evening meal will be provided at reasonable cost. Bookings are now being accepted and reservations will be made (subject to vacancies, upon application to The

Inset: Lord Vincent as a boy with two young friends 1943.
Right: House Mother Rules.

CHALICE WELL.
NOTICE.

GUESTS are requested
1. to retire in time to have lights extinguished by 11 p.m. [charge for gas 1/- per week per person]
2. not to leave gas burning in bedrooms.
3. To place hot water bottles [labelled] for filling, in Lobby [by Refectory] by 7.30 p.m. charge 6 per week.
4. To report all breakages to Warden or House Mother.
5. Not to gather flowers or fruit without permission.
6. To be quiet in house and garden between 2 and 4 p.m.
7. To tell the House Mother before 9. a.m. when they require sandwiches.
8. To be punctual for meals.
9. To enter their names & addresses in the Visitors book immediately on arrival.

The first bell is rung at 8.15 on weekdays & 8.45 am on Sundays. A warning bell is rung 15 minutes before lunch and supper.

WEEKDAYS		SUNDAYS
breakfast	8.30 a.m.	9 a.m.
lunch	1 p.m.	1 p.m.
Tea	4 p.m.	4.30 p.m.
Supper	7 p.m.	8 p.m.

Prayers are read in the Chapel immediately before breakfast and after supper each day.
Picture Post Cards can be obtained [price 2½ each] from Miss Hogg.

Warden.")

The early 1980's under the custodianship of Moya and Taras, saw modifications and improvements to Little St. Michael's including the creation of further bedrooms, bathrooms, a dining room and kitchen for guests use.

"In September 1984, Little St Michaels was opened again for Companions on a self-catering retreat basis. We have had quite a few Companions staying already and so far it is working very satisfactorily. All of us here enjoy having the opportunity to meet and get to know different Companions, while at the same time respecting the quiet retreat which everyone has come to experience.

It is a joy to prepare the rooms for each visitor and Merlene, Pip and Gladys have been such a wonderful help putting in many devoted hours of work. Those little extras mean so much.

The renovation and redecoration work is now finished in the kitchen and in two bathrooms. A third bathroom in the back overlooking Chalice Hill is well underway.

Many of the Companions who have already stayed here have blessed the Trust with suggestions, gifts and extra donations towards Little St. Michaels. All this has been so greatly appreciated; another affirmation of the love people have and how The Well is a part of us all" *Chalice Well Newsletter No. 5.*

A generous donation by John Rowntree in 1997, contributed towards the building of a timber-framed, glass-roofed meeting room adjacent to Little St. Michael's. Today, it is hired by a variety of groups and individuals from all over the world who offer training and workshops in healing, spiritual and personal development.

Chalice Well Retreat houses offer a quiet place to unwind for a few days. Comments in the guest books attest that there is something much more to get "in touch" with, and that "something" can be facilitated by being in a quiet setting, retreating from the chatter and noise of people and things.

"Chalice Well, sacred, beautiful place. How blessed we all are to have you. My heartfelt thank yous to all beings seen and unseen who make it such a magical healing place to be. So sad to leave, so wonderful to return" C Dixon

"A nurturing sacred space for a wonderful coming together of likened souls. A memory I will always treasure". T Ellis

"This has been a time to attune, to listen within and find deep peace. This place holds visions of what was, what is and what shall be". J Harding

Above top: One of the bedrooms in Little St. Michael's.
Above: Chalice Well Lodge.
Left: The Meeting Room.
Right: Little St. Michael's, Vine Cottage and May Cottage.

The Upper Room

Little St. Michael's Upper Room was created according to Tudor Pole's inspiration to provide a dedicated place for meditation, prayer and silent contemplation.

It was in a letter to Rosamond Lehmann on 1st March 1967 that Wellesley Tudor Pole first mentioned the idea of creating a room dedicated to prayer, silence and meditation: "our next task is to create an exact replica of our Lord's room within the 'Upper Room' at Little St. Michael's Retreat House. Simple, exact as possible and without any ecclesiastical trimmings." By this time the Trust had been running for approximately eight years, and a lot had been done to improve the spartan conditions encountered by housekeeper Christine Sandeman (neé Allen) in the early 1960's in the lower part of the house. But what had inspired Tudor Pole to embark on this project?

In 'The Silent Road' published in 1960 there had been a small chapter at the end of the book entitled 'Chalice Well and the Upper Room' which directed readers towards a booklet, one of the first published by the Chalice Well Trust, called 'The Upper Room with Commentary.' In this pamphlet Tudor Pole had pointed out that up until the Last Supper the feast of the Passover had always been kept as a thanksgiving for deliverance from evil, but after the Last Supper the feast was to establish a communion among humanity in joyful remembrance of the coming of a light into the world, a light "that so long as the earth remains will never be extinguished." He further writes that the man bearing the pitcher of water who guided the disciples to the original Upper Room is a symbol for the Aquarian Age. This figure appears on the cover of the pamphlet.

With the publication of 'A Man Seen Afar' in 1965, Tudor Pole placed another 'Upper Room' chapter close to the beginning of the book. Here Rosamond Lehmann writes, "a first reading of this chapter caused me to experience that kind of shock, as of inner recognition, that stills the

Left: Creation of Upper Room and roof repairs 1960's.

attention without conscious effort; and on a level that seems to make questions of 'evidence' or 'proof' irrelevant." She was referring to Tudor Pole's ability to glimpse or access memory and thus bring through to the present a memory of an event long passed. In a later book 'Writing on the Ground' Tudor Pole explained: "when one reaches up into the Spheres to grasp a fistful of ideas the results can be unexpected. One is not provided with a fluent stream of spiritualistic communications but with an assortment of symbols and hieroglyphics if you like, which at first glance mean nothing. In any case they are 'negatives' which must first be developed into three-dimensional positives. Quite an undertaking! Then comes the task of finding words into which the symbols can be clothed coherently."

Here we see Tudor Pole trying to convey the system by which he 'glimpsed' the past and the future and was able to externalise it into the present. There are many further examples of this work in all four of his books. With the Upper Room in Little St. Michael's the vision was clear. He would have probably drawn on the experience from 1909–1914 when he ran a guesthouse at 17, Royal York Crescent in Bristol. Here with Kitty, his sister, they turned a room at the top of the house into an Oratory where with the Allen sisters they held services, prayers, healings and viewings of the Bowl they had earlier found in Glastonbury. When his sister paid tribute to Wellesley in 'The Messenger' (an early version of *The Chalice*) of spring 1969, soon after his death, she refers to the Oratory as the "forerunner of the Upper Room!"

There were other ongoing examples of these dedicated rooms in existence. Grace and Ivan Cooke of White Eagle had published 'Healing' in 1955 in which the first chapter, 'The Story of an Upper Room' described such a room created in Kensington, London, where the windows are tinted with rose coloured glass. With blue walls it reflected an amethyst light around the room enhancing the healing sessions that took place there.

Another great soul of the twentieth century, Liebie Pugh, tells in her book 'Nothing Else Matters,' of the Gold Room in The White House in Surbiton, Surrey, as a place of sanctity and healing where there could be a "realisation of true being and communion with the divine." A contemporary of Tudor Pole, Ronald Heaver, had meanwhile created a sanctuary in Keinton Mandeville, Somerset, which is described in Allen Richardson's and Marcus Claridge's book about the inner work of William Grey. "Although its dimensions are not large from a physical view point," said Grey, "my immediate impression was that I had entered a vast cathedral. The spiritual structure of the location was overwhelming. It seemed to reach into the deepest recesses of one's soul."

It was thus to this type of dedicated sanctity that Tudor Pole turned when he began to create the Upper Room at Chalice Well. In March 1967 he

began his search for the furniture, the tables and chairs that would be needed for one end of the room. There is a wonderfully humorous account in 'My Dear Alexias' of his genie leading him to the perfect table in the cellar of a furniture repository only to find that the price was too high at £650.00. This led to him commissioning different people to construct what was needed. Richard Dell of Teignmouth made wooden cups, platters and bowls of a Jerusalem design in cherry wood. Ronald Parsons of Exeter carved a small receptacle in the shape of a fish for anointing purposes and John Shelly made the earthenware jugs. An expert wood carver and craftsman Edward Baly of Dartington built the table to specification, as well as a smaller serving table of yew.

By the end of April Tudor Pole wrote to Rosamond Lehmann that, "there is a presence already apparent in the room, now taking on it's destined shape and atmosphere. As a gesture to mark its inauguration I intend finding funds to provide an Indian village with water; this is also an expression of thankfulness for our own ever-flowing supply from our pure spring." This deep well was sunk in a village in Bihir province in Northern India. Tudor Pole hoped it would be one of many inspired by those who were to gain peace and vision in the Upper Room.

By August work was fully ongoing; the table was being made out of sycamore and the thirteen stools out of yew. These were completed by mid November. Tudor Pole asked Martin Israel if he would arrange the furniture at one end of the room which would also have a lamp burning continually in the window. The other half of the room was to contain chairs for meditation and a writing/reading desk facing towards the Tor. By December it was ready. "All went well on Monday and the Upper Room has now taken on an almost supernatural and strangely pervasive atmosphere," wrote Tudor Pole. "The table is finely proportioned, with a lovely sycamore top, and the stools of yew are completely right. M. Baly took especial care in carving the Masters stool [the only one with a backrest]." Present at the opening were Mr and Mrs Baly, with two of their craftsmen, Joy Mills, Kenneth Cumming, Chris Langlands and Mr and Mrs Simmons (the Wardens). Tudor Pole implies that after those attending had dedicated the room and retired downstairs for lunch a further ceremony took place during which "the custodian of the room was installed by an elder amidst an impressive concourse, comprehensive

Left: St. Michael sword carving.

beyond my expectations." There was a further session held over the Easter weekend 1968 with the laying of the table with meditative intent. The long raftered room sat under the roof and the windows now had amber glass (handmade by Jasper and Mollie Kettlewell), which filter through a golden light at all times of the day enhancing the peace and serenity. The room was divided in two by a light veil; the eastern end being for meditation, recuperation and restful thinking. The western end contained the scene as described in the booklet 'The Upper Room'. On the door was hung the St. Michael sword heraldic symbol. This is the drawing from which the carving was made for the Chapel at Iona. It depicts the hand of St. Michael holding aloft the shining blade of the spirit, with a hilt of gold, at the foot of which crouches the dragon, not killed, but transcended.

Undoubtedly the creation of this room ranks alongside the Silent Minute, the Lamplighter Movement and the securing of Chalice Well as one of Tudor Poles finest achievements. He was quick to make his views known about the future use of the room. "There can be no question of this room becoming a chapel, a conference hall, a lecture centre or a place where ecclesiastical services are held," he wrote in September 1967. "Its primary use should be as a centre for meditation, prayer and spiritual refreshment. This room is not intended to become a museum, a public library, a kind of Madame Tussauds, nor for use by groups of individuals engaged in special practices of their own, such as séances, yoga or occultism."

Over the years there have been many visitors to this refreshing oasis of the spirit. One such wrote in *The Messenger*: "We take ourselves momentarily through the veil as we relax into our time of mediation each in our own way and as we are accustomed … we do not just look at the scene, we become part of it. That is, as we might say today, attunement to the Wavelength of the eternal Christ, the same yesterday, today and forever. Is not this a supreme mystic experience?"

In 2007, it was finally time for Little St. Michaels to have a new roof. This undertaking had been delayed several times, partly because it would have meant interruption to the Upper Room. Much preparation both practical and meditative was undertaken before the work proceeded. The work was finished ahead of schedule, with the month of April having continuous blue skies; on Sunday 28th April LSM and the Upper Room was re-opened to guests.

In his third book 'Writing On The Ground' Tudor Pole was assisted by his friend, the cleric Walter Lang. Lang thought the idea of the Upper Room would smack of iconolatry, but that what he found there completely dispelled any doubts. "It seems clear," wrote Lang, "that what has taken shape in that room represents the external aspect of a spiritual energy so palpable that it registers on quite ordinary people, even those who are unaware of the background to the situation."

Lang then tantalisingly mentions a future possibility. "Believing the purpose of the Upper Room could not be concerned solely with providing a link – even a revitalised link – with the impulse of a passed or passing era I waited for an indication of some new factor suggesting a transition from the old to the forthcoming." The expectation of Walter Lang was realised at Companions Day 1967 when Tudor Pole introduced the idea of a future element to the room which would symbolise a breakfast. "In one room will be symbolised the alchemy whereby the Aquarian and the Piscean are reconciled. A healing presence," Tudor Pole went on, "dwells there which can be felt by those who know how to be inwardly receptive, a presence available for bringing harmony and health to those in need." He said that in due course a second table will eventually be laid for 'breakfast' at the end of the room facing the gardens and the orchards and across this scene the rising sun will cast its radiance.

Left: Lamplighter Light in West Window.
Above: Richard Dell's cherrywood cups and platters.
Overleaf: Upper Room.

Testimony: Personal Perspectives

No project or idea can become anchored in the physical world and then sustain over a period of fifty years without the creative, hard work of many, many people. This chapter is dedicated to all those who have played a part – some well known to us, some behind the scenes and some who wish to remain anonymous, working quietly away. So here we give 'glimpses' of the Chalice Well story through the voices and testimony of a selection of people who in some way were moved by what occurs here:

"The time was morning in April 1958, as we were about to drive home to Devon; the place by a gate in Wellhouse Lane, outside the Tor School, Glastonbury. A man came out from the house, and said 'Good morning.' He chatted for a moment, and then, unexpectedly, without preliminaries, he said he was troubled concerning the property of the Tor School. He told us he was the Headmaster, shortly to retire; he was anxious lest the property fall into the hands of those who had no reverence for the grounds in which lay the Chalice Well; he seemed seeking advice. My husband said 'Do you really want to be put in touch with the right man who can advise you?' 'Yes.' 'I think I can do that for you, I can contact Major W. Tudor Pole."

Later in this account:

"I saw the future pilgrims coming to Chalice Well, continuing the long chain of pilgrims of past centuries. They were coming from all quarters to a centre of healing of body, mind and soul. We Companions are privileged to play a part in this both now and in the years to come."

Companion Margaret R. Salmon from 'The Messenger' #1

"There is an air of purpose and enthusiasm at Chalice Well today which is reflected in the excellent progress I can report in the building of 'The Upper Room' in Little St. Michael's House, and on repairs and renovations to the property generally."

Warden John Simmons from 'The Messenger' #2

"Walking from the garden entrance above the Well in warm sunshine one was first impressed by a glow of colour, the scent of roses, the radiation of peace, and the greetings of friends. Companions rejoice to know that this long-cherished plan is now achieved. Many of us entered the Upper Room to 'Be Still' during the course of the day, and were aware of its blessing."

A West Country Companion from 'The Messenger #4

"Suddenly I was enveloped in a serene though vibrant golden light, and the whole landscape was lifted into a beauty past all description. A blessing was poured out from a cosmic source, and the creation was pervaded with the force of love. I knew at once that the malign influences that had not been completely transmuted had now been changed, and that the atmosphere had been cleansed. Truly, Chalice Well is a site of healing, a place of reconciliation and a beacon for the future."

In a letter from a Companion, M.S.I. in 1968.

"The Chalice Well Messenger arrived this morning (Nov.24, 1970). The date of postage on the envelope is October 12, 1970. One wonders where the mail has travelled when it takes so long, however we are not living in normal times so I guess we must consider ourselves lucky to receive it at all. I look forward to its coming. The peaceful vibration it brings does much to alleviate any inconvenience it may encounter along the way. I was born in England of Welsh extraction and lived in Aberystwyth for a number of years prior to leaving there in 1920.

Lots of water has flown under the bridge since then, but when 'The Messenger' comes its contents coincide with much of my ideas for the smallest thought of continuity of life after death is very helpful to me. This is my small world."

In a letter from Mary Myers, from 'The Messenger' 1971.

"In this way, such a place (i.e. of the Grail) is to be found at Glastonbury. It is the ancient Avalon, well known through the story of King Arthur and his Round Table. In a beautiful garden with many roses and all kinds of other flowers, there is a very old Well, the Chalice Well. Here the story is told about Joseph of Arimathea who came there after the crucifixion of Christ and poured His blood in the Well. Since that moment the water that comes out of it has a wonderful healing power."

From 'The Secret of the Grail' as written in 'The Messenger' #31 by a Rosicrucian visitor to Chalice Well from Holland, 1976.

"It is important that we make as conscious as we can the significance of this network of Light Centres, and co-ordinate them so that they can be a strong vehicle for the angelic forces to use. This is an aspect of the importance of Chalice Well."

Sir George Trevelyan, Companion's Day 1980.

"For those of us who are looking for a way to wake up the world, a haven becomes a very special place, a moment of peace and calm to reflect upon and refresh the higher vision of mankind. For those who are able to 'see' Chalice Well and drink of its spirit it is indeed a joy. There are few such special places in the world."

Brian Page Bauerle, a Companion from Thailand in Chalice Well newsletter 1983.

"Centres like Chalice Well exist that people may know the truth. The truth is that there is a spiritual existence that transcends and pervades the world of phenomenal beings. The world of spiritual reality is eternal and immortal. It can never be destroyed, just as we ourselves can never be annihilated in it. This is the function we Trustees and Workers have for Chalice Well, a place which will not depend on occultism, or prophecies or even astrology, but will depend on its own being, and will use all these things for the proper maturation of human nature. This to my mind really summarises the ideas of the healing mission of Chalice Well."

Trustee Dr. Martin Israel writing in Chalice Well newsletter #9.

"About Chalice Well itself. In the course of my own investigations, have I come across anything that could add to what I imagine all of you already know? One thing believed by many connected with Chalice Well is that the original Christian site in Glastonbury was up here rather than in the Abbey, that the story of Joseph of Arimathea relates to this area rather than down there. Nobody would dispute that the Old Church in the Abbey was very, very ancient, or that the religious community was very ancient – nobody disputes that at all. But some have believed that this was the first Christian site and Chalice Well was in a sense a holy well."

Geoffrey Ashe speaking at Companion's Day 1986.

"It seems to me that whatever goes on in places like Glastonbury, we need to encourage the notion of pilgrimage, and perhaps getting here is as difficult as actually arriving. The notion of pilgrimage is something we need to cherish, and develop and celebrate, and I think of that when I recall reading some information about Chalice Well, which says the place is here for healing, for nourishment, for strength, for peace. So thank you very much, Chalice Well, for what you do, and may you continue to do it for a very long time."

The Reverend Donald Reeves of St. James, Piccadilly at Companion's Day 1989.

"It was quite an experience draining the Well last November, venturing down the ladder to give it a cleaning. Entering the dark wet atmosphere of both underground chambers, where the water has been flowing unending for centuries, led me to wonder what journey it takes to reach here – where it starts, how far it comes, what stories it could tell!"

Ian Sargeant, Gardener, from the newsletter 1991.

"When you sit there (in Arthur's Courtyard) your chakras and etheric bodies, which are liable to be out of balance, are likely to be smoothed out by the earth energies present to restore you to a state of peace and harmony. I wish I could get all politicians, all big business men, and all leaders of armies to come to the Chalice Well garden for a few minutes every month, because their whole decision making process would be fundamentally altered."

Hamish Miller, from the newsletter 1992.

"Chalice Well rarely generates physical or emotional aggravations. It frequently brings peace and tranquillity to those who are traumatized or who are going through a long period of grief or emotionally heavy turmoil. It is as if it gives people indicating its symptoms space and time to 'breathe' emotionally while they go through a difficult time. Patients often return with a comment to the effect that they feel better able to cope and that they can see more clearly what they need to do. In those for whom it has been prescribed in high potency on mental/emotional indications of past trauma it may well give them 'voice' which if 'heard' will lead on to greater personal development."

Colin Griffith in "The New Materia Medica"

"In the 1960's Ann and I were lucky enough to see WTP give a talk at the Theosophical Society at Camberley in Surrey. Perhaps it was this, which led me to read one of his books. My expectations were wound up by the account of the Upper Room at Chalice Well and I was keen to visit. Armed with an introduction from Sir George Trevelyan we were welcomed by the Warden John Simmons in his green wellingtons, and shown upstairs. We went into the 'atmosphere', which was staggering and there on the table by the east window was the casket with the blue bowl. The experience was overwhelming. This was the early days when there were only a few hundred Companions and the bowl used to sit in the Upper Room. It was the major magic moment of my life. I can't remember anything else about that weekend!
Later I became a Companion and eventually a Trustee and Chairman of the Trust. There was a huge change over the years I was there from Leonard and Willa, through Fred and Colleen to Michael and Lynne. There has been a great expansion on all levels."

Roy Procter reflecting on his years of service to the Trust.

"The garden affects each one of us in a different way, some superficially, some deeply and lastingly. For me it is a constant source of wonder. Essences of the thousands of plants and flowers surround me with their healing nature. The birds and dragonflies come up to me as if to speak in an unknown language. Yet there is an understanding between us as we stare at each other in trust. One can see the change in visitors as they proceed through the garden. This is sacred. I am often asked, 'What is this place?' My answer is, 'Sacred.'

Guardian Colleen Heller-Rosado, 1998, writing in 'The Messenger.'

"Maybe many other people have had my wonderful experience at Chalice Well. About 15 years ago I took part in a Gatekeeper Trust West Country Pilgrimage with Sir George Trevelyan, Peter Dawkins and other lovely people. One of the first gatherings was round the Well for a meditation. I do not normally experience anything particular on these occasions. But I was extremely moved to receive the feeling coming from the Well of a deep, deep sadness, which I felt was due to the treatment of the Earth by humanity. There followed such an overwhelming wave of generosity that I have been led to work with several charities that care for this beautiful earth we live on."

Companion Joan Foden writing in 1999.

"Chalice Well is more than a place of spirituality, it has a power which you can only find and tap into if you are prepared to let yourself go. You don't, in my books, have to chant a mantra (though you might find it helps); you don't have to sit in the lotus position: you have to first acknowledge who and what you are, then allow the magic of the place to work. Listen to the sounds of water and wind, the songs of birds, the sigh of a breeze – all these help me and I am sure they would (help) you."

Alan Gloak, ex-Trustee and Chairman speaking in 2001.

"You can sit beside the well or on nearby seats. Often people have the experience here of the presence of a woman sitting by the well. She may be young or old, the Lover or the Hag herself. She is the Lady of the Well, the Lady of the Lake. Allow your mind to empty and look with you inner eyes to see if you can see her here. Listen for her voice on the breeze. Hear her words of wisdom."

**Kathy Jones in "In the Nature of Avalon;
Goddess Pilgrimages in Glastonbury's Sacred Landscape"**

"Chalice Well is like no other place. Sitting in the Gatehouse you could be suspended between Two Worlds. Not quite on the ground – not quite in the air.
So...who will come today?
The countless people who come to be held at an Inner Level whilst they work through grief, trauma, shock and massive life changes.
Those coming again and again to drink in the beauty, the peace, the sheer sacredness of the Avalonian Earth, Sky, Sun and Water.
The Garden calls people every day of the Year and even in the sleetiest, greyest weather there will be a steady trickle, little clusters, or a few solitary visitors. All of whom need to be in the Garden on That day. If we are called to be here, we come. Welcome.

Volunteer Susan M. Gibson in 'The Chalice' #19 2007

"While walking down the path between the chakra borders, the energetic presence translated into a silent chorus of hosannas. Drawn by the structure and form, colour and light, I was left in no doubt that I was accompanied by the Devic forces who dwell in the Chalice Well Gardens. The borders are a reflection of the tone, the note, the hidden music of Chalice Well. This silent leitmotif is available to be experienced in every tree, flower and shrub, in every summer shower or winter frost."

Companion Philomena Houlihan Wood in 'The Chalice' #18 2007

The Chalice Well at the Present Time

The administration of Chalice Well Trust has evolved over the years, adapting in response to experience and wider impulses. From one warden and a group of trustees (who were largely based in London), it first developed into a system comprising resident warden and many volunteers. Then came warden/guardians and the first paid staff. As the Trust grew so did the paid workforce. Towards the second half of the 1990's there was a big leap towards a staff team but still ably assisted by volunteers, who remain a mainstay of support to this day. Meanwhile the companionship grew steadily from several hundred in the 1960's to several thousand in the 1990's. By the middle of the first decade of this new century there had been six sets of guardians, who had lived and worked at Chalice Well.

The complexities and difficulties of this role had been recognised and it was decided to try a different system of working where management were not resident.

Living Intention

Today a circle of Trustees, Staff and Volunteers who fulfil the roles of governance, operational expertise and support, currently serve the Well. In recent years, the organisation has evolved from a traditional management structure towards what is described as a "flat hierarchy" model, where good communication and relationship is fundamental. Cooperation is induced through self-organisational teamwork and an engagement and participation in the decision-making processes. This is not regarded as new or radical as there are many organisations and community groups who are working in this way at this time. American Philosopher, William Irwin Thompson, describes this model as comprising spheres or circles of activity which all have a central point of reference.

For the Trust, this central point of reference is the Living Intention. This emerged during a period of change and transition from dialogue and discussions between Trustees and Staff. Co-Chair, Joanna Laxton

Opposite upper left and right:
gatehouse volunteers.
Below: Companions Day.
Above: Gathering at the Well
head, Easter 2008.

explained the Living Intention in the Companion's Journal "The Chalice".

"For those of us working at the Well our living intention must be to create the opportunities and atmosphere that can support individual and collective growth, through the practice of loving kindness, goodwill, and directed purpose in all our actions and interactions. The process of exploring such questions is moving us towards a greater unity, and a deeper understanding of our common purpose, which is to serve all those who visit and support this wonderful place. The experience is reshaping our actions and attitudes, both in the day-to-day running of the well and in our longer-term objectives."

Companions

This ethos of service extends itself to the companionship, which is a global community and network of support to which over 3,000 people currently belong. Many Companions connect with Chalice Well in their contemplative or spiritual practice and the Well continues to be a source of solace and inspiration. The Companionship not only provides spiritual

and energetic support but also a vital stream of income that contributes towards the fulfilment of the Trust's aims.

If the Well is held in the hearts and goodwill of the 'community of companions', then its spirit can express itself out from them into the wider world affecting others. The founder Tudor Pole believed that Chalice Well's existence is important for the world and humanity on a multitude of levels and many of the Well's Companions are working to engender positive change and evolution on a planetary level.

A "place for the healing of mind and body"

On Companions Day 1966, Tudor Pole stated "Chalice Well activities should give pride of place to the healing of mind and body through the agency of the Spirit with the co-operation of nature". Today, the activities, services and facilities provided by the Trust continue to hold true to this fundamental tenet.

The two retreat houses, Little St. Michael and Chalice Well Lodge,

provide a quiet and peaceful environment
in which to draw back from the busy-ness
of everyday life and take time to reflect
and be still. Providing retreat accommodation at the Well, allows the opportunity
for a fuller immersion into its energies
and many comment on a feeling of
wellbeing and a sense of "coming home"
during the course of their stay."

In Britain we are currently seeing an
exploration beyond organised religion in
a search for alternative and meaningful
ways to express and engage with spirit. At
Chalice Well, the gardens increasingly bear
witness to personal ceremonies such as
handfastings, marriage blessings, baby
naming and coming of age celebrations as
people choose to mark significant
moments in their lives in a place which
they hold as sacred.

The numbers of people attending the
Trust's programme of events and ceremonies are increasing and on occasion,
over 500 people have gathered to honour
the rhythms of the year and the turning of
the seasons in nature. These events have
become part of the calendar for the local
Glastonbury community while others
travel a considerable distance to attend.
These gatherings reflect a new and
emerging form of spiritual expression,
which is inclusive and universal in content
and language, and thereby open to all,
regardless of faith or spiritual path. The
ceremonies are grounded in common
principles; welcome, stillness, silence,

reflection, grace, communion, community, relationship, celebration, gratitude and blessing. That people gather together, not in a formalised building or structure of worship, but in a beautiful garden, allows a shared acknowledgement of the sacred and divine that transcends borders and differences.

The Trust 50th anniversary in 2009 afforded a wonderful opportunity to express and expand on this ethic through the over-lighting theme of "Many Paths, One Source".

Afterword

"To preserve in perpetuity the Chalice Well so the public may for ever have access to the intent that it may become a place of pilgrimage rest and recreation." *The Chalice Well Trust Declaration, January 1959*

The seeds for the future of the Chalice Well are sown in its past. This book is in part a story based on fact and actual events and in part a story not found in the pages of this book, but in its living spirit.

This living spirit which moves and touches with its grace and presence is expressed in the waters of the well that have flowed constant since the mists of time retaining their purity and vitality. Chalice Well is not immune from the vicissitudes of every day and world events, as we have seen in this written history. The world does come through its gates, and those who have lived and worked here have often reflected that it is not always an easy or comfortable place to be. It is a living sanctuary and to maintain and preserve the dynamic, nurturing creative energy and timeless separateness that is here requires great heart.

Many of the world's great teachers, for example the Dalai Lama have experienced times of turbulence and difficulty which have affected the journey of their lives and yet, they understand peace as a state of being. When times are unsettling and disturbing, to have a tranquil place in which to sit as if "in the eye of the storm" is beneficial and offers the possibility of another way.

Holding Chalice Well as a living sanctuary is important not only for those who need to come to a place that reflects peace and wellbeing, but also for those who do not or cannot come. It is significant simply because it exists. There are many places of beauty and transcendence in this world. Nature has always been available for humanity to connect to, but Chalice Well is one of a number of places on the planet that are consciously held to enable and facilitate this connection. The story of Chalice Well is about a response to a Spirit or presence of place, which fulfils a human need to touch and be touched by a source. There is a strong relationship between the place and those who are holding it as sacred. This is a place where Spirit has and continues to be recognised and it is this spirit that informs its activities and relationships. The vision for Chalice Well embraces a vision for a new world, a world where spiritual and material dimensions meet and are indistinguishable and indivisible. This new world is not so different from the world in which our ancestors lived, knowing that all things were intimately connected and all came from the Source. Tudor

May Day celebrations.

Pole wrote of a vision where humanity ceases to hang itself upon a cross of suffering and instead sips the cup of Joy. This cup of joy heralds a return to an original and true state of human beingness. If Chalice Well is seen as an allegory for the paradisal Garden of Eden, then perhaps humanity never left the garden and our return is simply a remembering of where we have always been.

Previous Page: Children floating candles on Halloween. Tim Wheater and Natalie Shaw in concert.

Selective Bibliography

Introduction

John Michell, 'New Light on the Ancient Mystery of Glastonbury', Gothic Image 1990
Anthony Roberts Ed., 'Glastonbury, Ancient Avalon, New Jerusalem', Rider 1978

Chapter 1 –From the Mists of Time

Geoffrey Ashe, 'Avalonian Quest', London, 1982.
William Camden, 'Britannia', trans., Philemon Holland, 1607.
Dion Fortune, 'Avalon of the Heart', Aquarian Press, 1934/1971.
Philip Rahtz, 'Glastonbury', London, 1993.
George Wright, 'The History of Glastonbury During the Last Forty Years,' Bulleids of Glastonbury, Armynell Goodall, Taunton, 1896.

Chapter 2 – Alice Buckton

Abdu'l-Bahá in London: 'Addresses and Notes of Conversations', Bahá'í Publishing Trust, 1987
Patrick Benham, 'The Avalonians', Gothic Image, 1993
Tracy Cutting, 'Beneath the Silent Tor', Appleseed Press, 2004
J.E. Esslemont, 'Bahá'u'lláh and the New Era: An Introduction to the Bahá'í faith', Bahá'í Publishing Trust, 1950, 1970, 1976, 1980.
Violet M. Firth, 'Avalon of the Heart', Frederick Muller, 1934

Rosemary Harris, 'The Chalice Well Newsletter' (No.2), 1982
Anjam Khursheed, 'The Seven Candles of Unity: The Story of 'Abdu'l-Bahá in Edinburgh', Bahá'í Publishing Trust, 1991
Irene M. Lilley, 'Friedrich Froebel: A Selection from his Writings', Cambridge University Press, 1967
Robert Bernard Martin, 'Tennyson: The Unquiet Heart', Faber & Faber, 1980
Editor Norman Page, 'Tennyson: Interviews and Recollections', Macmillan, 1983
Peter Smith, 'A Concise Encyclopedia of the Bahá'í Faith', Oneworld Publications, 2000
Bob Trotter, 'The Hilltop Writers', The Book Guild Ltd., 1996
The Chalice Well Trust, 'The Chalice: Journal of the Companions of the Chalice Well', Issue No 19, Summer 2007
Basil Wilberforce, 'G.W.E. Russell', John Murray, 1917

Chapter 3 – Wellesley Tudor Pole

Neville Armstrong (ed.), 'Harvest of Light', Neville Spearman, 1967 .
Patrick Benham, 'The Avalonians', Gothic Image Publishing, 1993/2006.
Andrew Dakers, 'Big Ben Minute', Andrew Dakers Ltd., 1942
Rosamund Lehmann, 'Harvest of Light', 1976
Sir David Russell Special Collection   St. Andrews University, Fife, Scotland.
Chalice Well Trust, 'Collection of Wellesley Tudor Pole

Writings & Leaflets', Glastonbury.
Wellesley Tudor Pole, 'The Mind Set Free', Watkins,
1960
Wellesley Tudor Pole, 'The Silent Road: In the Light of
Personal Experience', Neville Spearman, 1960
Wellesley Tudor Pole, 'A Message For the Coming
Time', Big Ben Council, 1962.
Wellesley Tudor Pole, 'Private Dowding', Pilgrim Book
Services, 1966 .
Wellesley Tudor Pole, 'The Upper Room
Commentary', Chalice Well Trust/Devonshire Press,
1968.
Wellesley Tudor Pole, 'Writing On The Ground',
Neville Spearman, 1968.
Wellesley Tudor Pole, 'My Dear Alexias' (Letters from
Wellesley Tudor Pole to Rosamond Lehmann), Neville
Spearman, 1979.
Wellesley Tudor Pole & Rosamond Lehmann, 'A Man
Seen Afar', C.W. Daniels, 1965.
Oliver G.Villiers, 'Wellesley Tudor Pole: Appreciation
and Valuation', Chalice Well Trust.

Chapter 4 – The Trust

Patrick Benham, 1993/2006, ibid.
Peter Caddy, 'Perfect Timing', Findhorn Press, 1996.
Tracy Cutting, 'Beneath the Silent Tor: The Life and
Work of Alice Buckton', Appleseed Press, 2004.
Felicity Hardcastle, 'A Short History of Chalice Well',
Chalice Well Trust, 1962.
Sir George Trevelyan, 'Summons To A High Crusade',
Findhorn Press, 1986
Chalice Well Trust Newsletters & Bulletins:
1959 – 1967 misc. from Chalice Well Trust Archive.
1967 – 1979, The Messenger of the Chalice Well (38 issues).
1981 – 1996, The Chalice Well Newsletter (19 issues).
1998 – 1999, Chalice Well Messenger (2 issues).
1999 – 2008, The Chalice (23 issues, ongoing).
Oliver. G.Villiers, 'Marching Forward', Chalice Well
Trust Archive.

Chapter 5 - The Gardens

Time line: Researched by Ark Redwood, Chalice Well
Newsletters 1967 – 2008 ibid.
Felicity Hardcastle, ibid. 1962
The Inner Garden: Cynthia Sandys & Rosamond
Lehmann, 'The Awakening Letters', Neville Spearman,
1978.
Kathy Jones, 'In the Nature of Avalon', Ariadne
Publications, 2000.
Richard Leviton, Looking for Arthur, Station Hill
Openings, 1997.
Nicholas R. Mann, 'The Isle of Avalon', Green Magic,
1996/2001.

Paul Broadhurst & Hamish Miller, 'The Sun and the
Serpent', Pendragon Press, 1989.
John Michell, 'City of Revelation', Abacus, 1973.
Oliver. L. Reiser, 'This Holyest Erthe', Perennial Books,
1974.
Wellesley Tudor Pole, ibid. 1979

Chapter 6 - The Waters

Dr. F. Batmanghelidj, 'Your Body's Many Cries for
Water', The Tagman Press, 2000.
Janet & Colin Bord, 'Sacred Waters: Holy Wells and

Water Lore in Britain and Ireland', Granada, 1985.
Celtic Connections: The Journal of Celtic Culture and Related Subjects, Vol. 1. Dec. 1992.
Masaru Emoto, 'Love Thyself: The Message from Water III', Hay House Inc., 2004
Masaru Emoto, 'The Secret Life of Water', Simon and Schuster UK Ltd., 2006
Madeleine Evans, 'Meditative Provings: Notes on the meditative provings of New Remedies', The Rose Press, 2000.
Alexa Fleckenstein, 'Health2O: Tap into the Healing Powers of Water', McGraw Hill, 2007
J. M. Harte, 'The Holy Wells of Somerset':
http://people.bath.ac.uk/liskmj/living-spring/sourcearchive/fs2/fs2jh1.htm
Chögyam, Ngakpa and Déchen, Khandro, 'Spectrum of Ecstasy: Embracing the Five Wisdom Emotions of Vajrayana Buddhism', Shambhala, 1997.
Alexander Lauterwasser, 'Water Sound Images', Macromedia Publishing, 2006.
Alan Levett, 'The Cress Field,' The Messenger, February 1999, No. 21.
Rev. Lionel Smithett Lewis, 'Glastonbury: Her Saints AD 37-1539', St. Stephen's Press, 1925.
Sig Lonegren, 'Spiritual Dowsing', Gothic Image, 1986.
Nicholas R. Mann, 'Energy Secrets of Glastonbury Tor', Green Magic, 2004.
Hamish Miller & Paul Broadhurst, ibid. 1989
Ann Procter, (Ed.), 'This Enchanting Place: Facets of Chalice Well', Chalice Well Trust, 2006.
Viktor Schauberger, Translated & edited by Callum Coats, 'The Water Wizard: The Extraordinary Properties of Natural Water', Gateway, 1997.
Theodor Schwenk, 'Sensitive Chaos', London, Rudolf Steiner Press, 1965.
Wellesley Tudor Pole, 'The Healing Properties of Spring Water', Chalice Well Archives, 1948.

Helen C. Watling, 'Sacred Springs/Holy Wells,' Celtic Connections, Issue 21, Winter 1997.
Wells Journal, 16 & 24 June and 12 July 1921 & 7 July 1922.
John Wilkes, 2003, Flowforms: The Rhythmic Power of Water, Floris Books.
Holy Wells Index:
http://people.bath.ac.uk/liskmj/wells/index.htm
Institut für Strömungswissenschaften, Herrischried:
http://www.stroemungsinstitut.de/prospect.htm

Chapter 7 – The Buildings

Felicity Hardcastle – "The Chalice Well; A Short History", Chalice Well Trust, 1962
Rupert Sheldrake – summary of "Morphic Resonance" found in his glossary at
http://www.sheldrake.org/glossary/
National Archives, Somerset Record and Archive Service - Glastonbury documents,
DD\SAS\C/795/SE/8 1733 – 1848
Glastonbury Antiquarian Society, 1799 George Cox Survey; 1844 Glastonbury Tythe Survey, http://glastonburyantiquarians.org
1891, 1901 Census – The National Archives
The Catholic Encyclopedia, Vol XIII, Caxton Publishing Company, London, 1912.
The Chalice Well No.1 4, Newsletter, 1984
The Messenger, Journal No. 29

Acknowledgements

We first have to thank Natasha Wardle and Paul Fletcher for the vision and original intention of the book. Subsequently they have given many hours researching, writing, co-operating, selecting photographs and seeing it through to completion.

Natasha and Paul would like to thank Angela Marsh at Ziggurat Design for her patience and understanding, and Robert Grocott also at Ziggurat for his sympathetic layout and design which brings the book to life.

Many others have also contributed in writing, editing and constructing the book. Particular thanks go to Nicholas Mann and Caroline Sherwood for their work on the Mists of Time, Alice Buckton and Water chapters, Hamish Miller for the Foreword. Thanks to Joanna Laxton for her support, encouragement and input to the editing process.

Thanks to Jenny White, Ark Redwood, Anthony Ward, Caroline Wyndham, Alan Levett, Alexander Lauterwasser, Ann Procter, Gabriella Gabrielle, Ned Reiter, Sig Lonegren, Somerset Library Service and the staff of Glastonbury Library, Sophie Knock of Avalon Flower Essences, Sylvia Francke, Tracy Cutting, Godfrey Bishop, Steve Atkinson archivist at Theatre Royal Haymarket London, Christopher Hawkes Curator of Wells Museum and Mrs Edith Kenney, for their work and input in particular chapters.

We would also like to thank all those in previous years who had the wisdom and foresight to archive the materials, particular mention goes to Tim Hopkinson-Ball, Alan Royce and William Carroll assisted by others who catalogued and sorted through many of the Trusts Papers and to Paul Fletcher for his current stewardship of the Archives. Thanks also to Moira McKenzie and the staff at the Russell Special Collection at St. Andrews University, Scotland.

Thanks to the Reverend Canon Anthony Harding for his information on John Power and the Missionary of the Sacred Heart and also David Bromwich of Somerset Studies Library who assisted with census searches.

For the excellent photography we thank Tony Arihanto, Saul Macauley Haines, Helen Megginson, Palden Jenkins, Catherine Wixey, Nicholas Mann, Michael Orchard, Rob Parry and Ann Cook. Thanks also go to Johannes Fehr who scanned many of the Trust's Archive photographs for this publication.

Special thanks to the proofreaders for their sterling attention to detail.

We thank the previous Guardians for leaving a record of their activities and thank those Guardians who are still around for their contemporary memories of their time at the Well in a series of interviews given to Paul Fletcher.

We thank all the Trustees, Staff, Volunteers and Companions past and present who have given their support and service to the Chalice Well throughout the last 50 years.

Special thanks go to the current Trustees for their incredible support for this book.

Finally of course we thank our founder Wellesley Tudor Pole for his remarkable vision and constant energy in establishing the Chalice Well Trust. He believed in the spiritual outpouring of this era that is represented by the child of the union between cosmic and primeval divine wisdom, and the equally important power of eternal and all embracing love.

This book is dedicated to this anchoring principle.

Picture Credits

Alexander Lauterwasser, Water Sound Images in a "well", www.wasserkloangbilder.de

Glastonbury Antiquarian Society; 1799 George Cox Survey, Map of Glastonbury

Jamie George & Frances Howard-Gordon – Gothic Image Publications, The Allen Sisters.
Basil Wilberforce

National Portrait Gallery, London, Alfred Lord Tennyson by James Mudd

Rural Life Museum, Alice Buckton & Friends

University of St Andrews Library; The Omphalos, from the North East, the Great Palace, Istanbul (Constantinople) (ref: ms38515-13-5-169), General view of the Byzantine mosaic from the North East Colonnade of the Peristyle colonnade, the Great Palace, Istanbul (Constantinople)(ref: ms38515-13-5-127)

Other photographs by; Tony Arihanto, Saul Haines, Michelle Scott Macauley, Helen Megginson, Rob Parry, Palden Jenkins, Catherine Wixey, Michael Orchard, Nicholas Mann and Ann Cook.

All other pictures copyright the Archives of the Chalice Well Trust.

Note: We apologise, if we have missed any picture credits and please contact the Chalice Well Trust so that you can be credited in future editions.

If you wish to support and uphold this living sanctuary, you can become a Companion of Chalice Well. The companionship annual subscription is a vital source of income for the Trust and contributes to the daily running costs of the gardens, the charity and its works.
For further information or for General Enquiries, Please contact:

The Chalice Well Trust
Chilkwell Street
Glastonbury
Somerset
BA6 8DD

(+44) 01458 831154

email: info@chalicewell.org.uk
www.chalicewell.org.uk

INDEX